THE COMPLETE CHEESE COOKBOOK

Other books by Judy Ridgway

The Vegetable Year Cookbook
Frying Tonight
Man in the Kitchen (with Alan Curthoys)
The Little Bean Book
The Little Lemon Book
The Little Rice Book

THE
COMPLETE
CHEESE
COOKBOOK

Judy Ridgway

 PIATKUS

Copyright © 1986 Judy Ridgway

First published in 1986 by
Judy Piatkus (Publishers) Ltd of
5 Windmill Street, London W1P 1HS

British Library Cataloguing in Publication Data

Ridgway, Judy
  The complete cheese cookbook.
  1. Cookery (Cheese)
  I. Title
  641.6′73   TX759
  ISBN 0-86188-398-5

Edited by Susan Fleming
Designed by Susan Ryall
Special artwork by Linda Broad

Phototypeset in 11/13pt Linotron Times
Printed and made in Great Britain by
The Bath Press, Avon

My thanks to Jackie Gordon and Kate Frears
for all their help in testing the recipes.

CONTENTS

CONTENTS

LIST OF ILLUSTRATIONS

Cheese means different things to different people: in Holland it means a sliceable cheese for eating at breakfast and at snack meals; in India it means a home-made curd cheese to be curried; and in France it means a range of cheeses so large that there's a different one for every day of the year! In the English speaking world, cheese means a range of locally made cheese, some specific to their own county, others derived from immigrants. It is Europe that has largely been the home of cheese-making, and its influence has reached to almost all the cheese-eating countries of the world.

In Britain today, we are able to buy most of the major – as well as a large selection of the minor – cheeses of the world. With such a choice on supermarket shelves, and with specialist cheese shops scattered around the country, it's easy to choose an array of quite different cheeses for a first class cheeseboard.

What is less easy, however, is the question of how to use the cheeses up after the cheeseboard has been discarded. Some will, of course, be eaten up in sandwiches, on salads or at snack meals, but in my experience there are always some cheeses which sit in the fridge in their clingfilm until they go mouldy. But those days are now over, and I positively welcome the rather oddly shaped pieces of cheese left over from dinner parties or wine and cheese parties.

The reason is that I cook with them. Small pieces of blue cheese brighten up sauces and quiches; goat's cheese adds interest to green salads or fruit and cheese starters; and the smelliest of soft mature cheeses can transform cheese canapés. Once I started, I found that the ways in which even the most esoteric cheese could be used were almost endless. There are many classic dishes which use cheese, and though these usually specify a particular cheese, I found that other cheeses could quite easily be substituted. The purists may say that the result is not the same but I say, from some experience, that they are usually very good despite the results being slightly different.

This book, then, is not a treatise on how cheese is made or a guide to the cheeses of the world – there are some very good books on these subjects already on the market – but rather a guide to cooking with cheese; all cheese. The choice of cheeses is a personal one. It is probably not completely comprehensive: there is bound to be the odd cheese here and there which has been imported by an enthusiast! However, all the generally available cheeses have been included and there are certainly enough of the more unusual ones to act as an introduction to the enormous present-day choice. I have listed selected cheeses alphabetically at the beginning of each section, and the letters against the names refer to the likely availability of the cheese;

(E): Easily available in most supermarkets and shops selling cheese.
(S): Available in large supermarkets, specialist delicatessen counters and cheese shops.
(L): Locally available only; either in the country of origin or in the small area around the farm in which it is made.

Some cheeses are particularly good for cooking; some are thought to be unsuitable. But if the way each cheese will behave on heating and cooking is taken into account, they can all be pressed into service. Thus I have divided the cheeses into groups according to their composition and the way in which they behave in cooking, rather than on scientific, national or bureaucratic criteria. The hard cheeses are grouped together, as are the blue cheeses, goat's cheeses etc, and any of the cheeses listed in the introduction to a section can be used in any of the recipes in that section. In some instances, however, I have suggested specific cheeses. This is either because the dish is classically made with the cheese or because I have had particularly good results with that cheese. But that does not mean you cannot use another cheese of the same type.

Indeed the idea of the book is that you should be able to find a recipe to use up whatever cheese you happen to have left over. There is no reason why you should not experiment with different cheeses within the sections and in some instances across the sections. In fact this is exactly what I hope will happen! May you have lots of success!

Cheese-making is one of the oldest forms of food-manufacture, and dates back at least 5,000 years to Ancient Sumeria. Remains of cheese-making equipment have also been found in Ancient Egypt and in Bronze Age Britain. How cheese-making actually started, though, is shrouded in the mists of time, but any community which kept herds of milk-producing animals was likely to discover cheese in due course. For if milk is left to stand for any length of time it will go sour and separate into curds and whey. This is due to the action of a bacterium which feeds on the sugar in milk and forms lactic acid in its place; once the lactic acid reaches a certain level the milk protein, casein, will separate from the watery contents.

The first cheeses were made by drawing off the whey from the curds of soured milk. The curds may well have been squeezed by hand to facilitate the escape of the liquid. They were then eaten fresh, but were soon also shaped into cakes and left to dry. Drier cheese had the advantage of keeping for longer.

The next step forward in cheese-making was the discovery of agents which would speed up the souring and curdling process. Acids such as lemon juice and vinegar were both used in this connection, and indeed are still used today in the production of some fresh cheeses. However, rather more important was the discovery of enzymic curdling agents for sweet milk. The best known is rennet, produced in the fourth stomach of young cud-chewing animals. However, plant juices were also used, and these included thistle and safflower juice and the juice of ladies' bed-straw, which used to be called 'cheese rennet' by country people. The importance of these enzymic agents was that they produced a different kind of fermentation from lactic fermentation. This gives a totally different kind of cheese. In addition the enzymes could continue to work in the cheese over a long period and thus ripen it. This meant that cheese could now be made in summer when the milk-producing animals were grazing well, and could be kept into the winter when milk would be scarce.

Early cheeses were made mainly from goat's and ewe's milk. Cattle tended to need too much grazing and were too expensive for many communities to keep. In Mongolia, mares were milked, and in other areas buffalo and llama were pressed into service. As communities grew richer so more cow's milk cheese appeared.

By Greek and Roman times, a high degree of sophistication had been reached in cheese-making. There were many different kinds of cheese, some using salt to draw out the moisture, and others flavoured with all kinds of herbs and spices. Fresh cheese was still eaten at home but hard cheese was made to store and to use for travelling. The Roman legions, for example, were issued with a small portion of cheese a day and it is possible that it was the legionnaires and then the later settlers who introduced cheese-making to the rest of Europe. Some of these European cheeses were held in such high esteem that they were sent back to Rome: the British Cheshire cheese is believed to have been among those favoured!

Originally cheese was eaten on its own or with bread. The Romans were the first to record the use of cheese in cookery. Hard cheeses were sliced into salads, and cheese was mixed with flour, eggs and oil, and the resultant cakes baked in the ashes and coals on the hearth. The softer fresh curd cheeses were used in mixtures with meat or fish, hard-boiled eggs and herbs. Cheese was also used in all kinds of pies and pastries.

But cheese-making hardly survived the decline and fall of the Roman Empire. Standards fell and then the Barbarian hordes over-ran the area – and they were not cheese-eaters! Recipes and techniques were largely forgotten, surviving only in the monasteries. But by medieval times cheese was again being produced in some quantity. Fresh cheese made from full-fat milk or from cream was reserved for the rich; peasants had to rely on skimmed milk and this made a very hard cheese which was not popular with the better-off. Essex and Suffolk cheeses, for example, were so hard that a rude rhyme was written about them:

'Those that made me were uncivil,
They made me harder than the devil.
Knives won't cut me, fire won't sweat me,
Dogs bark at me, but can't eat me.'

Those with their own goat or sheep may have had some fresh cheese, but even here there was more of a need to make hard cheeses to keep for the winter.

By Tudor times, though, the British cheeses we know today were beginning to emerge. At first each farm made its own cheese, with each one different from the other. But gradually farmers would club together, or a large landowner's bailiff would manage the production of all the cheese on the estate, and a distinctive and consistent flavour and texture was achieved.

Cheddar was one of the first. It was probably made with ewe's milk in the beginning, but then came to be made with cow's milk. Throughout the centuries Cheddar has maintained its popularity, and many other countries have copied the 'Cheddaring' techniques of milling and double scalding the curd – the hallmark of a Cheddar. Cheshire was another early cheese, with a history going back to before the Dark Ages. By the seventeenth century there were noted cheeses from various counties and these were offered for sale at cheese fairs such as Stourbridge, Bulford,

Weighill and Atherstone. As these cheese markets gained in importance, so merchants, factors and pedlars bought up cheese for resale in other parts of the country. Towards the end of the eighteenth century the cheese managers of London formed themselves into an unofficial guild and their factors toured the country looking for good cheeses.

Development of cheese-making in Europe followed a similar course. Gorgonzola and Parmesan in Tuscany, and the French Brie, Cantal, Roquefort and Comté were among the first European cheeses to emerge. A Dutch cheese (known as 'deadman's head' for its characteristically round shape) and Gruyère in Switzerland were among the forerunners. Many of these cheeses travelled well beyond their own countries. Parmesan was considered by the wealthy to be the best of all cheeses in sixteenth-century England. Old Dutch cheese came next in popularity, with English cheese a poor third.

As in pre-history the early European cheese revival produced cheese which was mainly eaten on its own or with bread. It was known as 'white meat' and was considered to be an adequate substitute for meat and fish for the poor. However, toasted cheese was very popular in Elizabethan times. One recipe mixed chopped asparagus and ham with onions, anchovies and melted cheese. This concoction was spread on toast and grilled again. Potted cheese soaked in wine was also very popular.

By the seventeenth century the European influence started to extend the use of cheese in cooking. The French had been using it for a long time to flavour various hashes of meat and vegetables, then to flavour their sauces and later, more sophisticated dishes. In Italy cheese was used extensively with pasta, and macaroni cheese was to become an English favourite.

The emigration of Europeans to the North American continent meant that a wide variety of cheese-making techniques went with them. However, these were extremely local in scope and it wasn't until the middle of the nineteenth century that the first factory making cheese on a large scale was opened in New York State. It was exclusively devoted to the production of Cheddar. Many of the native American cheeses such as Colby, Coon, Monterey and Tillamook are based on Cheddar.

Back in the UK, a disastrous outbreak of cattle disease in 1860 and the subsequent drastic fall in milk production led to an influx of American cheeses. Local cheese production, which had already started to decline with the onset of the Industrial Revolution, fell even further. In an attempt to restore the tradition of English cheese-making the first UK cheese factory was opened in 1870, and by 1878 factories had spread, and were being established in other major cheese-producing counties.

Factory-made cheese – or, to give it its modern name, creamery-made cheese – now accounts for 90 per cent of all cheese production in the UK. The percentage of creamery-made cheese is also high in the other European countries and in the United States. Little changed in the cheese-making world until the Second World War when cheese production in the UK was curtailed and 'uniform' cheese production became obligatory. It was not until 1950 that real attention could again be given to the development of county cheeses. The English Cheese Council was established in 1955 and their job was to promote the nine English county cheeses: Caerphilly, Cheshire, Cheddar, Double Gloucester, Derby, Lancashire, Leicester, Stilton and Wensleydale.

With the exception of Stilton, these cheeses may be made by creameries in any part of the country and they carry a cheese mark to show that they are up to specified standards of quality, again with the exception of Stilton. In addition some cheeses may carry English Farmhouse cheese labelling. This means that the cheeses have actually been made on the farm rather than in a factory or creamery. These include the nine English county cheeses, but also a whole range of other cheeses which are made and distributed locally.

Among the English cheeses only one, Stilton, carries its own specific Certification Trade Mark. The mark ensures that this cheese is made only in Leicestershire, Nottinghamshire and Derbyshire, and that only the old-established method is used.

Certain other European cheeses are subject to an agreement which defines the cheeses and stipulates the conditions under which their name may be used. For example, a Brie-style cheese must come from France and a Cheddar-style cheese from England: if it does not, then the name of the country of origin must be attached to the name of the cheese – Bavaria Brie or New Zealand Cheddar, for instance.

There is also a further more exacting control on certain cheeses which ensures that cheese called by a particular name may only come from where that cheese traditionally originated. Cheeses which carry the *appellation d'origine* are Bleu d'Avergne, France; Brie de Meaux, France; Comté, France; Gorgonzola, Italy; Livarot, France; Munster, France; Neufchâtel, France; Parmesan, Italy; Pecorino Siciliano, Italy; Pont l'Evêque, France; and Reblochon, France. Thus, any cheese labelled Parmesan must come from the Parma area of Italy.

Cheese is often high on the list of those high-fat foods which, it is suggested by modern nutritionists, should be reduced in the diet. While it is perfectly true that most cheeses do have a relatively high fat content – around 40–50 per cent – there is no reason why they should not form an important part of a balanced diet. If you are in the habit of eating cheese in addition to a protein-rich meal of meat or fish, then cheese is certainly an indulgence, but it may be used as a useful alternative to meat or fish in much the same way as it was in the past.

In fact cheese is not a very significant factor in the UK diet. The average consumption is only about 3½–4 oz/90–100 g a week. The only people who might be at risk from a high cheese consumption are those who have a known heart condition, and who have been advised to switch to a special diet – for cheese does contain cholesterol. And, of course, its fat content, being of animal origin, is saturated. But many fresh cheeses, such as cottage cheese, are made with skimmed milk and these together with low-fat quark and the special fat-reduced cheeses have very much less fat than the average cheese. Some kinds of quark and fromage frais have virtually no fat.

Most cheeses are also good sources of protein, the only exception being cream-based cheeses. Cheddar, for example, contains about a quarter of its weight as protein. Calcium, phosphorus and some other minerals are found in cheese – about 2 oz/50 g Cheddar or Parmesan cheese can supply the adult recommended intake of calcium. However, fresh soft cheeses and all cheeses formed from lactic fermentation lose some of their calcium with the whey.

Vitamins in cheese include the Vitamin B complex and Vitamin A as well as D and E. Vitamin C is lacking in all cheeses, and Vitamin A is lost to those cheeses made from skimmed milk.

Cheese has an unfounded reputation for

CALORIE CHART FOR COMMON CHEESES
1 oz/25 g cheese

Austrian Smoked	78
Babybel	97
Bel Paese	96
Boursin	116
Bresse Bleu	80
Brie	88
Caerphilly	120
Camembert	78
Cheddar	120
Cheshire	110
Cotswold	105
Cottage cheese	30
Cream cheese	125
Curd cheese	40
Danbo	98
Danish Blue	103
Derby	110
Dolcelatte	100
Edam	88
Emmental	118
Feta	54
Gorgonzola	100
Gouda	100
Gruyère	132
Halloumi	84
Lancashire	109
Leicester	105
Lymeswold	105
Parmesan	105
Port Salut	94
Quark, skimmed milk	25–40
Roquefort	88
Stilton	130
Wensleydale	115
White Stilton	96

being indigestible. This idea arose in the sixteenth and seventeenth centuries when doctors advised the rich against the consumption of hard cheese saying that it was fit only for the poor who had of necessity stronger stomachs! Uncooked cheese is certainly not indigestible, but its fat content does mean that it remains in the stomach for longer than carbohydrate foods. This fact probably led to the idea that cheese eaten late at night would cause nightmares. When cheese is cooked it tends to become harder and less digestible, but this does not occur in sauces or in any dish where the cheese is combined with a starchy food to prevent the separation of the fat. Nor does purely melted cheese cause indigestion for this has not reached the temperature required to separate and harden it. The important point to remember about cheese is not to *over*-cook it.

Uncooked cheese may be served as one course of a main meal or it may form the basis of the main course of a light or snack meal, or even breakfast. It all depends where in the world you are!

The first great bone of contention about serving a cheese course is when it should be served. In Britain it is usually served at the end of the meal. This is probably a reflection of the fact that in Georgian times the upper classes believed that cheese 'closed the stomach' at night after the day's food and drink, and in particular after all the claret they had drunk. In France the custom is to serve the cheese after the main course and vegetables but before the dessert. This too probably reflects their concern about wine: in this case not its digestibility, but the fact that the palate cannot appreciate the sort of good red wine the French like to serve with the cheese course if it has already had to deal with a sweet dessert. In Portugal, cheese is often eaten before the meal as an appetizer, and in Greece the cheese is served with the meal as a side dish and can be eaten at any time. In Scandinavia, Germany and Holland, cheese is served for breakfast.

The form is which the cheese is served also varies for it may be placed in large chunks on a cheeseboard for everyone to help themselves, or it may be sliced and then served. However, this is usually a function of the meal and the type of cheese being served. The cheeses served for breakfast in Holland, for example, are usually beautifully and thinly sliced with a Continental cheese slicer.

Accompaniments to the cheese also vary both from cheese to cheese and from country to country. Celery and grapes have become standard almost everywhere, and all kinds of salad ingredients may also be pressed into service. Special accompaniments include mustard with Gruyère, pears with Gorgonzola,

caraway seeds with Munster, and apple pie with Wensleydale.

Some cheeses are usually served on their own, others are used mainly in cooking. However, there are no hard and fast rules and if you like a cheese there is no reason why you should not include it in a cheeseboard selection – Parmesan, for instance, is quite delicious and different eaten in a chunk rather than grated on pasta.

PLOUGHMAN'S LUNCHES

The traditional ploughman's lunch of a piece of hard cheese and a hunk of bread has turned into the rather more sophisticated 'pub' lunch of a choice of cheese, rolls or French bread, butter, tomato, pickles and perhaps a lettuce leaf or two.

Here are some ideas for ringing the changes on the traditional Ploughman's Lunch:

AUSTRIAN PLOUGHMAN

hunks of rye bread
thick round of Austrian Smoked cheese
1 portion sliced cucumber in vinegar
3–4 spring onions (scallions)

COMMON MARKET PLOUGHMAN

small pieces of French bread
1 wholemeal roll
butter
small chunks of French walnut cheese,
    German Edelpiltzkäse,
    Italian Bel Paese, English Derby
1 pickled cucumber
1 tomato

FRENCH PLOUGHMAN

lengths of buttered French bread
large slice of Brie or 2 quarters of Camembert
4–6 cocktail gherkins
½ large Continental tomato
1 head chicory (endive)

GERMAN PLOUGHMAN

small hunk of rye bread
2 slices pimpernickel
thinly sliced Tilsit and a piece of Bavaria Blue
1 pickled cucumber, sliced
1 tomato

GLOUCESTER PLOUGHMAN

buttered wholemeal rolls
chunk of Double Gloucester or Cotswold cheese
3 pickled walnuts
chunk of cucumber
lettuce leaves

IRISH PLOUGHMAN

hunks of buttered soda bread
chunk of Irish Cheddar
1 portion potato salad
1 tomato
lettuce leaves

LEICESTER PLOUGHMAN

hunks of granary bread
chunks of Stilton or Leicester cheese
pickled onions or piccalilli
1 tomato
lettuce leaves

SCOTTISH PLOUGHMAN

1 slice wholemeal bread
2 oatcakes
butter
chunk of Dunlop or Orkney cheese

1 tomato
lettuce leaves

WELSH PLOUGHMAN

hunks of buttered cob loaf
chunk of Caerphilly cheese
3 pickled onions
1 tomato

YORKSHIRE PLOUGHMAN

buttered wholemeal bread
chunk of Wensleydale cheese
1 sliced green apple
1 tomato
1 portion chutney

CHEESEBOARDS

A good cheeseboard is one of the marks of a good host or hostess. The selection should be made bearing the following points in mind: colour, texture and flavour.

Colour is always extremely important in presentation and a cheeseboard with all the cheeses looking the same will not be very attractive. This is true even if the individual cheeses taste quite different. So choose one or two well coloured cheeses or one with a brightly coloured rind. Parsley, watercress and grapes can also be used to add extra colour.

Different textures, both in the rind and the paste of the cheeses adds interest to the board. Include both hard and soft cheeses and perhaps a cheese with large or small holes. A blue cheese should be included both for its texture and colour and for its flavour.

Last, but by no means least, choose a variety of different flavours. Some people prefer very mild or buttery flavours; others like a salty cheese; and others again enjoy the pungent flavour of a well matured cheese or a goat's cheese. Arrange the milder cheeses together, moving across or round the board for the stronger cheeses.

Set the cheeses out on a cheeseboard with one or two cheese knives and cover with clingfilm or a glass globe. Cheese will keep fresh like this for an hour or two. If you are planning to store the cheese for a longer period under the globe add a lump of sugar to absorb the moisture which will evaporate from the cheese.

Some people like to mix cheeses from many countries, others like to stick to one country alone. However, it is easy to get carried away when selecting and buying cheeses for a cheeseboard. But it is really only sensible to balance the numbers who will be served with the number of cheeses that will be sufficient to give a reasonable choice. Don't buy too large pieces if you are offering a selection. On the other hand some people like to offer just one or two cheeses such as a whole Brie or a large piece of Reblochon and one of Roquefort.

Here are some interesting combinations to try:

Boursin
Camembert
Gouda with caraway seeds
Dolcelatte

Brie
Mature Cheddar
Gorgonzola
Pyramid Chèvre

Bel Paese
Pont l'Evêque
Jarlsberg
Banon
Blue Cheshire

Munster
Bleu d'Auvergne
Tilsit
Sainte-Maure
Wensleydale

Chabichou
Saint Paulin
Reblochon
Taleggio
Lancashire
Stilton

Appenzell
Livarot
Roquefort
Herb Roulé
Demi-Sel
Doux de Montagne

WINE AND CHEESE PARTIES

A wine and cheese party is both easy to prepare and very enjoyable – for both guests and host. There is very little preparation and no cooking to worry about. Everything can be prepared in advance and there isn't much clearing up afterwards. The cheeseboards should follow the same principles as those set out in the previous section, but you may like to put all the mild, strong and blue cheeses each on their own boards. Pieces of cheese of about $\frac{1}{2}$ lb/225 g are probably the smallest you can effectively display, and eight $\frac{1}{2}$ lb/225 g blocks will serve sixteen to twenty people. Do remember to label the cheeses. You can either buy special flags or simply write on sticky labels and wrap one end round cocktail sticks. (If you do not have enough cheese, chopping and bread boards, you can press baking trays and serving trays lined with foil into service to hold the cheese. The foil can then be used to wrap up any leftover cheese.)

Bread and butter are essential accompaniments. Substantial chunks of a variety of breads add to the festive appearance of the table. Choose from French sticks, Vienna loaves, Danish rye bread, English cottage or granary and wholemeal bread. A basket of mixed crisp and soft rolls also adds interest. Have several dishes of butter so that it can be reached easily when everyone crowds round the table. Blocks of butter are perfectly adequate, but if you have time you might like to mould butter in some traditionally patterned moulds or make some old-fashioned butter rolls.

Vases or jugs with sticks of celery can also be dotted around the table. Indeed all kinds of raw fruits and vegetables go well with cheese: offer sticks of carrots, wedges of fennel, sliced chicory heads, radishes, spring onions, cauliflower florets, or green and red pepper rings. If you make your own chutney or pickles, this would be a good time to show them off!

The choice of wines is very much a matter of your own preferences, but some people like to stick with cheeses and wines from the same country. Some white and some red wine should be provided to allow for different tastes. Remember to chill white wine for an hour in advance in the fridge, but don't over-chill or the wine will lose some of its flavour. Red wines should be served at room temperature but this does not mean keeping them in a hot kitchen. The ideal temperature at which to serve most red wines is 20–21°C/68–70°F. Exceptions are some of the new young wines such as Beaujolais Nouveau which come on to the market in the late autumn and which should be lightly chilled. Most modest red wines are improved by being opened for an hour or two. This gives them time to breathe – get some air to the wine.

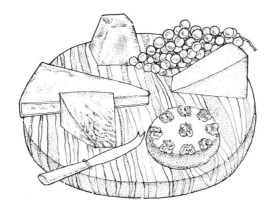

Some cheeses are particularly suited to cooking. These are the ones which grate or crumble easily, and soft fresh cheeses which simply melt into almost any medium. However, you can cook with any kind of cheese, and one of the purposes of this book is to show how small amounts of leftover cheese can be used up effectively in cooking.

The list of uses of cheese in cooking is almost endless. It can be sliced, cubed or grated and used in salads, fruit and cheese medleys and in cold canapés. It can form the basis of a hot snack or be used to flavour pasta and egg dishes. It can also be used to enhance meat and fish dishes and to flavour and give body to soups, sauces, flan fillings and pastry. Cheese also makes a good topping for vegetable dishes. It can simply be sprinkled on at the last minute and allowed to melt or it can be mixed with breadcrumbs and scattered over the top before going into the oven or under the grill.

As mentioned earlier, cheese cooked on its own can separate and harden. However, if you follow a few basic rules all will be well.

1. Don't apply too much heat for too long a time.
2. Where possible, mix the cheese with a starchy food such as flour or breadcrumbs.
3. Grate hard cheese fairly finely for adding to cooked dishes.
4. Only cook sauces or soups long enough to melt the cheese.

While I would argue that most cheese can be used in most dishes it is true that certain types of cheese are better in certain applications than others. Sometimes you need a good melting variety which does not pull into threads; on other occasions quite the opposite is required. Sometimes you need a cheese which does not fully melt; on other occasions it is the strength or piquancy of flavour which is most important. In this connection it is worth remembering that blue cheese seems to intensify in flavour on cooking. Surprisingly this does not happen to goat's cheese which actually loses a little of its musty flavour.

Unless otherwise stated, most of the following recipes serve four people.

HARD CHEESES

All these cheeses will grate well and can be used in cooking in much the same ways as you would use the best known of them, such as Cheddar, Gruyère and Emmental. Of course there will be differences in both the texture and the flavour of the finished dish: some cheeses go much more stringy on cooking than others, for example, and the stronger cheeses will impart a much more strongly cheesy flavour. However, it's quite simple to cut or increase the amount of cheese used in a recipe by a fraction, and this sort of change will not affect the success of the dish.

Buying Guide

The golden rule with all cheese is to buy it in as fresh a state as possible, so start by buying only from those shops which have a high turnover at the cheese counter. Secondly, try only to buy cheese which is freshly cut from the whole cheese. Cheese which has been cut and wrapped by the shop or has been vacuum-packed will simply not taste the same. The next point to look out for is the labelling. Fresh Farmhouse cheeses are usually labelled as such and some French cheeses carry an official 'appellation d'origine' declaration on their packaging. Finally, an examination of the cheese itself will show you whether or not it is in good condition. It should not show any signs of drying up, nor should it be 'weeping' in any way. The rind, if there is one, should be dry.

Storing Guide

Double-wrap all cheese by wrapping first in clingfilm or foil and then place in a polythene bag. Keep in a cool place or in the base or vegetable box of the fridge.

Most cheese will keep for a week or two but some of them will mature to a stronger tasting cheese. Others such as Caerphilly should be eaten fairly soon after purchase.

Indeed it is best where possible only to buy sufficient cheese for your immediate needs.

If you do not have a fridge, store in a cool food cupboard or a cellar. The temperature should not exceed 10°C/50°F. Try wrapping in foil and storing in an earthenware crock on a tiled or marbled floor.

All cheese can be frozen but those with a medium- to low-fat content will start to crumble on thawing. These cheeses are best frozen grated and this can also be very useful for the busy cook. The younger, less mature cheeses also tend to lose flavour in the freezer. High-fat cheeses can be frozen very successfully, but they should all be eaten within 2–3 months. Thaw at room temperature and store in the fridge. Use within 3 or 4 days of thawing. Double wrap, first in clingfilm and then in foil. This stops the salt in the cheese coming into contact with the foil.

Slicing and Serving

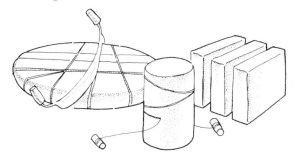

CAERPHILLY *(E)*: This is more correctly classified as a semi-hard cheese, but it will not slice with a Continental cheese slicer and so I have left it in the hard cheese section. The cheese was originally made in Wales but is now made in South West England. It is only matured for about a couple of weeks and has a clean and mild, but quite distinctive, flavour. The cheese is quite large and has a smooth white mould. Eat fairly soon after purchase.

CANTAL *(S)*: This large French cheese, probably the oldest of the French cheeses, is made in the Auvergne. It has a thickish rind and has a fairly strong distinctive flavour.

CHEDDAR *(E)*: This is *the* universal cheese. It was originally made in the Mendip hills close to the Cheddar Gorge, but it is now made all over the world and, unless the cheese carries an English cheese mark on it, it may have come from almost anywhere between Ireland and New Zealand. It may be mild or pronounced in flavour depending on how long it has been matured. Some very mature cheeses are particularly strong. The paste is cream to deep yellow in colour depending on the state of maturity.

Its many variants include the following:

Cheddington: Cheddar with horseradish and dill
Cheviot: Cheddar with chives
Ilchester: Cheddar with port wine
       Cheddar with sweet pickle
       Cheddar with beer, garlic and parsley
       Cheddar with sage
Nutcracker: Cheddar with walnuts
Nutwood: Cheddar with cider, hazelnuts (filberts) and raisins
Rutland: Cheddar with beer, garlic and parsley
Windsor Red: Cheddar veined with elderberry wine

CHESHIRE *(E)*: This is one of the oldest of the English Farmhouse cheeses. It has a mild and mellow flavour, with a touch of saltiness in the younger cheeses. There are both red and white versions. The younger cheeses have a characteristic crumbly texture.

COLBY *(L)*: This cheese was created in Wisconsin in the United States by a special process which lowers the temperature of the curd during curing. The cheese is deep yellow-orange and is either waxed or vacuum-packed. The flavour is sweet and mild.

COMTÉ *(S)*: This is a French cheese rather similar to Emmental. It comes in large discs and has a thick hard rind and a pale yellow paste with scattered holes. It will grate and slice and is particularly good for cooking.

CORNISH YARG *(L)*: This new English cheese has a clean, mild flavour. It has a dark mould rind which is coloured by the nettle leaves in which it is wrapped while maturing.

CUMBERLAND FARMHOUSE *(L)*: Made localy in small quantities. This is a semi-hard cheese with a golden yellow colour and a mellow flavour. The cheese is lightly waxed.

DERBY *(S)*: This is a close-textured English cheese which is mild and slightly tangy when young but which develops a much fuller flavour as it matures. At Christmas the cheese used to be flavoured with sage leaves but Sage Derby is now available all the year round.

DOUBLE GLOUCESTER *(E)*: This traditional English Farmhouse cheese has a very smooth close texture with a full mellow flavour. The paste has a deep golden straw colour. The word 'double' in its name refers to the old practice of using full-cream milk from two milkings. Double Gloucester also used to be twice the size of Single Gloucester cheese which was made with a mixture of skimmed evening and morning milk.

Its many variants include the following:

Cotswold: Double Gloucester with chives and onions
Ilchester: Double Gloucester with onions and chives
Peppervale: Double Gloucester with

chopped green and red peppers
Sherwood: Double Gloucester with sweet pickle

DUNLOP *(L)*: This traditional Scottish cheese is rather similar to Cheddar but perhaps slightly softer and more mellow.

EMMENTAL *(E)*: This is one of the oldest of Swiss cheeses and is probably imitated as much as Cheddar. It has a rich creamy-yellow colour, and a sweet, subtle, almost nutty flavour. It has large holes distributed throughout the paste, and some of the cheeses can be huge. No Emmental less than 4 months old may be exported, and at this stage it is still regarded as a young cheese. In the US, however, it is sold and eaten at this age, but in Europe people tend to choose older cheeses up to 10 months old. The German version of Emmental is known as Allgau Emmental. Emmental is used widely in cooking of all kinds.

FONTINA *(S)*: Genuine Fontina comes only from Val d'Aosta in the Alps, near the Italian borders with France and Switzerland. The rind is uneven and light brown in colour. The paste is pale straw-coloured and slightly elastic with small round holes. The flavour is a little like Swiss Gruyère but rather sweeter.

GRUYÈRE *(S)*: This is Switzerland's best cheese. It is a smaller cheese than Emmental and has a creamier texture and smaller holes. It is not such a spectacular cheese as Emmental but it has a mild cheesy flavour which strengthens on cooking. It has been used in most classic French and English cooking for a couple of centuries.

There are French and other versions of the cheese, notably Gruyère de Beaufort and Gruyère de Comté. These are sometimes known simply as Beaufort or Comté.

KEFALOTIRI *(S)*: This Cypriot cheese was originally circular, and a mixture of ewe's and goat's milk. It is white and salty to the taste. However, it has a much finer texture than Feta cheese which it resembles slightly.

LANCASHIRE *(E)*: This cheese has a very soft white crumbly texture but is also quite creamy. It can be strong or mild in flavour depending on how long it has been matured. Nowadays it is usually sold young but in its native county the mature version has always been preferred. It is sometimes flavoured with sage.

LEICESTER *(E)*: Shaped like a large millstone, this cheese is coloured to a russet orange. It has a medium strong flavour and fairly granular texture. It is sometimes known as Red Leicester.

ORKNEY *(S)*: This is another traditional Scottish Farmhouse cheese which is now made in the creamery. It usually comes as whole small round cheeses. They may be red or white or smoked. Sold young it is closely textured and flakey.

OXFORD *(S)*: This relative newcomer to the market is based on a cheese which was made until the middle of the last century. The cheese has a good flavour and a smooth texture.

PARMESAN *(E)*: This extremely close-textured hard Italian cheese is used in many international classic dishes. The whole cheese is an enormous pale brown drum and the paste is straw-yellow and slightly grainy. It makes a good dessert cheese when young and then matures to provide a hard cheese which will grate extremely finely and give an excellent flavour to all cooked dishes. It is often sold ready-grated in tubs but the product bears little relation to freshly grated Parmesan.

PECORINO *(S)*: This is another really hard Italian cheese. In Italy it is almost as popular as Parmesan but it is much more difficult to obtain elsewhere. It is traditionally made from ewe's milk and is used in much the same way as Parmesan.

PROVOLONE *(S)*: This Italian cheese takes its name from a round local cheese which used to be called Provra. Manufacture of Provolone has spread to the US and to Latin America. The cheese may be young and mild or well matured with a sharper flavour. It has a thin golden-yellow rind, and small cracks start to appear in the paste as the cheese matures.

WENSLEYDALE *(E)*: Like Lancashire, this cheese is fairly crusty. It has a good flavour and an almost honey-like after-taste.

WHITE STILTON *(E)*: This crumbly white version of Stilton has a sharp, fairly acid flavour, somewhat akin to Feta cheese. It is sold after only 8 weeks. If it is kept for longer it will naturally start to grow a blue mould resulting in a rather milder cheese than the regular Blue Stilton.

Smoked Cheeses

APPLEWOOD *(S)*: This is a delicately smoked Cheddar cheese which has been rolled in paprika.

CHARNWOOD *(S)*: This is another smoked Cheddar with paprika.

CUMBERLAND SMOKED CHEDDAR *(L)*: This is a farm-matured cheese which is smoked over oak shavings to give a smooth and delicate flavour.

GERMAN/AUSTRIAN SMOKED CHEESE *(E)*: These are long sausage-shaped processed cheeses which are mildly smoked and encased in a plastic wrapper.

Fat-Reduced Cheeses

The following are available under various brand names:

CHEDDAR
CHESHIRE
BLUE TENDALE

There is also a range of flavoured cheeses which contain half the fat of normal Cheddar:

ABBEYDALE – with onions and chives
ALBANY – with celery seeds
GROSVENOR – with mixed herbs
PENMILL – with peppercorns.

SEMI-HARD OR SLICEABLE CHEESES

In practice there is often a very fine dividing line between a hard and a semi-hard or sliceable cheese. It is, after all, possible to slice many of the hard cheeses, and the semi-hard cheeses can mostly be grated and used in just the same way in cooking as hard cheeses. But in this book I am concerned mainly with the culinary uses of cheese, and so have ignored the scientific classifications: instead I have made a sometimes arbitrary division between the two classifications. However, all the cheeses in this section, with the exception perhaps of Mozzarella, have that sort of waxy texture which can be very thinly sliced with a Continental cheese slicer.

For culinary purposes most semi-hard cheeses can be used as hard cheese and so

I have not devised a separate recipe section for them.

Buying Guide

Choose freshly cut cheese. Avoid cheeses which are drying up at the edges or on the cut surface. The waxy texture should be smooth and glossy and free from any exudation of fat.

Storing Guide

This kind of cheese keeps very well. Wrap in foil or clingfilm and place in a polythene bag. Keep at the bottom of the fridge for up to 2–3 weeks. Remove about 30 minutes before eating. To freeze, slice and store double-wrapped between sheets of clingfilm. Thaw at room temperature within 3–4 months. Use within a week of thawing.

Slicing and Serving

This type of cheese lends itself particularly well to slicing. The best implement to use is a Continental cheese slicer. This looks rather like a short cake slice with a slit across the blade by the handle. To slice the cheese simply draw the slice across the surface of the cheese and thin slices of cheese will come off.

APPENZELL (S): This Swiss cheese undergoes a unique curing process which gives it a pronounced aroma and fairly strong piquant flavour. During curing, the cheese is immersed for several days in a vat of white wine or cider and water with spices and herbs. The amber-coloured paste is smooth and dense with a few pea-sized holes scattered through it, and the rind is hard and thick.

BABYBEL (S): The small whole cheeses are the French version of the Dutch Edam. They have the same red wax covering and smooth pale yellow paste.

BELLE DES CHAMPS (S): See Soft Matured Cheeses.

BELLSHIRE (S): See Fresh Soft Cheeses.

BRICK (L): This American cheese was first created in Wisconsin and owes its name to the shape of the cheese. Its texture is similar to Tilsit or Port Salut. The rind is reddish in colour. The cheese has a sweet spicy flavour.

CHAUMES (S): Made in the foothills of the Pyrenees this medium-sized round French cheese has small holes in the paste. It has a yellow-orange rind and a rich mellow flavour. The cheese can be sliced, but it behaves very like a soft matured cheese on cooking.

DANBO (E): A mild Danish cheese similar to Samsø, but it is often paler in colour. The cheese is square in shape with a slightly nutty flavour. It can be sliced or grated. There is also a version which is flavoured with caraway seeds.

DOUX DE MONTAGNE (E): This mild French cheese has a few small holes in the paste and is plastic coated in light brown to give it the appearance of a country cob. It has a distinctive buttery flavour.

EDAM (E): This is one of the most popular of Dutch cheeses. It has a fairly low fat content and is sold young. It has a bright red wax coating and the paste is yellow and smooth. It can be sliced or grated.

ESROM (S): This thin-rinded very mild Danish cheese is square in shape and the paste is full of small holes.

FETA (E): In its native Greece the cheese is usually made from ewe's milk but elsewhere it is made from cow's milk. It is white in colour and has a sharp salty flavour. It is crumbly in texture and is stored in brine.

GOUDA *(E)*: This Dutch cheese is similar to Edam but the paste is slightly softer and more waxy, and it has a hard yellow waxy rind. The flavour is fairly mild. Mature Gouda has a stronger, more piquant flavour, and a darker harder paste. There is also a version with caraway seeds and another with cloves.

HALLOUMI *(E)*: A semi-hard cheese from Cyprus which can be sliced but not crumbled. It is made from ewe's milk. It has no rind and is kept in whey brine. It is usually sold in rectangular blocks in sealed packs with its own whey brine. When cooked this cheese seizes up and goes tough rather than runs and should not be cooked for too long.

HVARTI *(S)*: This cheese is very similar to Esrom but is rectangular in shape. There is also a small round version which is rindless and creamier.

JARLSBERG *(S)*: This Norwegian cheese is based on an old recipe. The cheese has an elastic texture rather like Gouda. It has a mellow, slightly sweet flavour, and a golden-yellow paste with variously sized round holes. It can be used for all kinds of cooking.

MESOST *(S)*: This Swedish cheese is made by boiling whey until all the liquid has been evaporated. The resulting solids are pressed and made into a form of cheese. It is butterscotch in colour and has a very distinctive flavour.

MONTEREY *(L)*: This cheese is popular throughout the United States and Canada. It may be disc-shaped or oblong with a thin rind and a mild and buttery creamy-coloured paste. It is also known as Jack or Monterey Jack.

MOZZARELLA *(E)*: This is actually a spun-curd soft cheese made originally in Southern Italy from buffalo milk. The cheese ripens very rapidly and should be eaten fairly quickly. It is stored in brine, pure white in colour and has a very bland flavour. It can be sliced, and goes extremely stringy on cooking. Italian Mozzarella cheeses are small and round. Imitations are made from cow's milk and are often oblong in shape. In the US these blocks are known as pizza cheese. Real Buffalo Mozzarella has a stronger flavour but is more difficult to find.

PORT SALUT *(S)*: This cheese was originally made by the monks of the Abbey of Port du Salut but the name was sold to a large French cheese manufacturer. The cheese has a tawny washed rind and smooth, springy pale yellow paste.

PYRÉNÉES *(S)*: This French cheese has a distinctive black-waxed coating. The cheese is medium-sized and round. The flavour is mild and nutty.

SAINT ALBRAY *(E)*: See Soft Matured Cheeses.

SAINT/ST PAULIN *(E)*: This cheese is derived from and is very similar to Port Salut. It has the same bright orange rind and the cheese itself is mild. It is available in wedges or as small round whole cheeses.

SAMSØ *(E)*: Denmark's national cheese is not unlike Cheddar in flavour. It can be coarsely grated or thinly sliced. It has the odd small hole in the paste, and is fairly mild.

SVENBO *(S)*: This Danish cheese is dry and yellow in colour with numerous large holes. It may be round and coated in yellow paraffin wax, or it may be rectangular and uncoated. It has a characteristic sweetish taste.

TILSIT *(S)*: This mild German slicing cheese is pale golden in colour and has tiny holes distributed throughout the paste.

TOMME DE SAVOIE *(S)*: This medium-sized cheese is a speciality of the Haute-Savoie in France, and it is also made in Italy. The taste is slightly acid and aromatic.

SNACKS, APPETIZERS AND CANAPÉS

Potted Cheese

Potted cheese is unusual nowadays but eighteenth-century cooks often used the technique to brighten up old cheese or to keep cheese for a little longer. Old recipes vary in the alcohol and spicing used and some even used sugar; so if you find any of the mixtures a little bitter, try adding a teaspoon of icing sugar to each 1 lb/450 g of cheese used.

This recipe traditionally uses Cheshire cheese but any kind of hard cheese can be used. Serve on fingers of toast or canapés, or use in sandwiches.
See also page 87 for Potted Blue Cheese.

6 oz/176 g hard cheese
3 oz/75 g ($\frac{1}{3}$ cup) butter
1 tablespoon dry or sweet sherry, or white wine
pinch of mace, nutmeg or mustard powder

Grate the cheese, using a finer mesh for harder, less crumbly cheeses. Melt the butter and pour about 2 oz/50 g on to the cheese. Keep the rest warm to pour over at the end. Add the sherry or wine and the spice. Mix well together to form a smooth paste. Press into one or two small pots. Chill for 20 minutes and then pour on the rest of the melted butter. For a smoother effect clarify the remaining butter before pouring over the potted cheese. Keep in the fridge for up to 3 weeks.

Cheddar and Corn Potato Topping

Cheese makes a particularly good topping for jacket-baked potatoes. Use any grated hard cheese on its own or, for a change, try this unusual mixture, in which I used Cheddar. (See also Soft Cheese recipes for more potato toppings.)

2 spring onions (scallions)
1 × 7 oz/198 g can (2 cups) sweetcorn niblets
2 tablespoons milk
6 oz/175 g (1½ cups) hard cheese, grated
4 jacket potatoes, baked in the oven

Slice the spring onions and place in a saucepan with the sweetcorn, its juice, and the milk. Heat gently, then add grated cheese and cook until the cheese has melted and the sauce is hot. Cut a cross in the top of each potato and spoon over the topping.

Mozzarella and Salami Sandwich

Any kind of sliced sausage or ham can be used in place of salami.

4 slices rye bread
2 oz/50 g (¼ cup) butter
¼ cucumber, sliced
1 Mozzarella cheese, sliced
4 slices peppered salami
8 tablespoons coleslaw salad
1 box mustard and cress
4 small radish roses

Spread rye bread slices with butter and arrange the cucumber slices over them. Place the cheese slices on the bread to cover cucumber. Cut the slices of salami in half to give eight half-moon shapes and place at either end of the bread with rounded edge outwards. Place the coleslaw in the gap between the moons and garnish with a small bunch of mustard and cress and a radish rose.

Welsh Rarebit

This is one of the English classics, and I usually make it with Cheddar. It makes an excellent snack. Place a poached egg on top to make Buck Rarebit.

½ oz/15 g (2 tsp) butter
2 tablespoons (3 tbsp) brown ale
1 teaspoon dry mustard powder
8 oz/225 g (2 cups) hard cheese, grated
ground black pepper
dash of Tabasco (optional)
4 slices bread

Place the butter in a small saucepan with the brown ale, dry mustard and cheese. Heat gently over a low heat, stirring occasionally, until the cheese has melted. Add pepper to taste and Tabasco, if used. Meanwhile, toast the bread lightly on both sides and when the cheese has melted, divide the mixture between the slices of toast. Place under the grill and grill for 1–2 minutes until bubbling and light golden brown. Serve with pickle.

Croque Monsieur

This is the French version of cheese on toast. Use a stringy cheese like Gruyère or Emmental if you can.

8 slices white bread, crusts removed
3 oz/75 g (⅓ cup) butter
4 slices ham
4 oz/100 g (¼ lb) hard cheese

Butter all eight slices of bread lightly, using about a third of the butter and cover four of them with ham. Cut the cheese into thin slices and cover the ham. Top with the remaining bread slices and press sandwiches together. Spread top of each sandwich with butter and cook under a medium grill for about 3 minutes until golden brown. Turn sandwiches over, spread with butter and then cook under the grill for another 3 minutes until golden. Serve at once. Alternatively, fry in a non-stick pan on both sides.

Roast Cheese

This easy-to-make snack originated in Georgian England. It was served as a late evening snack and could be made by a kitchenmaid, or cook boy after the chief cook had retired for the night. Today it still makes a good supper snack, or it can be cut into squares or triangles to be served as hot canapés. Use the egg white left over to make Swiss Cheese Croquettes (see page 43).

1 egg yolk
1 oz/25 g (1½ tbsp) butter, softened
2 oz/50 g (1 cup) fresh white breadcrumbs
2 oz/50 g (½ cup) firm English cheese, grated
pinch of dry mustard powder or a few drops Worcestershire sauce
salt and pepper
4 slices bread, toasted
1 tomato, sliced

Mix the egg yolk, butter, breadcrumbs, cheese, mustard and seasoning to form a smooth paste. Spread this mixture over the toast making sure it goes right up to the edges. Place on a baking tray and bake at 200°C/400°F/Gas 6 until the cheese mixture melts and begins to bubble. Finish off under a hot grill. Top with a slice of tomato.

Right: *Mature Soft Cheese Selection (top) and English Blue Cheeses (below).*

Mexican Huasvucli

This was a traditional dish to serve during Holy Week; however, it makes a very good snack at any time. Serve also with fingers of brown toast as an unusual dinner-party starter. I usually make it with Cheddar, but it is equally good with many other hard cheeses.

4 tomatoes, peeled, seeded and chopped
4 oz/100 g ($\frac{1}{2}$ cup) butter
salt and pepper
pinch of chilli powder
4 eggs
4 oz/100 g (1 cup) hard cheese, grated

Fry the tomatoes in the butter with the seasonings. Break the eggs into the pan and stir a little. Add the grated cheese and continue cooking, stirring from time to time until the eggs set.

Gruyère Moons

This deliciously rich version of cheese straws comes from Switzerland. They make an excellent party snack served warm or cold.

6 oz/175 g (1 cup) flour
6 oz/175 g ($\frac{3}{4}$ cup) unsalted butter, softened
6 oz/175 g ($1\frac{1}{2}$ cups) grated Gruyère cheese
1 egg
salt to taste
few grains cayenne pepper
1 egg yolk

Mix together the flour and butter, and work in the cheese, egg and seasoning. Mix to a soft dough.

Cut the dough into two equal portions and leave one portion chilled while rolling the other. Roll out the dough to $\frac{1}{8}$ inch/3 mm thick on a well-floured surface. Cut into circles with a tumbler, then cut into each circle to make a half-moon shape. Re-roll all the trimmings and re-cut. Repeat until all the dough is used. Place on a lightly greased and floured baking tray and brush with egg yolk. Bake in a preheated oven at 180°C/350°F/Gas 4 for 8 minutes.

Use the second portion of dough in the same way.

Left: *English Hard Cheeses (top) and Goat's Cheese Selection (below).*

Planked Eggs

These little potato nests used to be baked on a wooden plank which was taken straight to the table. Any hard cheese is good.

$1\frac{1}{2}$ lb/675 g potatoes, peeled and cut into chunks
2 tablespoons (3 tbsp) milk
salt and pepper
4 tomatoes, skinned and sliced
4 large eggs
3 oz/75 g ($\frac{3}{4}$ cup) hard cheese, grated
1 tablespoon freshly chopped chives or spring onions (scallions)
1 tablespoon freshly chopped parsley
1 oz/25 g ($1\frac{1}{2}$ tbsp) butter

Boil the potatoes in the usual way. Drain well and mash with milk and seasoning. Pipe into four nests on a heat-proof plate. Arrange the tomato slices in the base of the nests. Next break an egg into the base of each nest. Sprinkle with cheese, chives or spring onions and parsley, and dot with butter. Bake at 180°C/350°F/Gas 4 for 15 minutes.

Scotch Cheese Eggs

This cheesy version of Scotch eggs can be served hot or cold. Use Dunlop for a traditional flavour.

8 oz/225 g (2 cups) hard cheese, grated
2 eggs
freshly ground black pepper
3 oz/75 g ($1\frac{1}{2}$ cups) fresh breadcrumbs
4 hard-boiled eggs, peeled
1 oz/25 g ($\frac{1}{2}$ cup) dry breadcrumbs
oil for frying

Mix the cheese with one of the eggs, pepper and sufficient fresh breadcrumbs to make a pliable dough. Leave to rest in a cool place for 30 minutes. Roll out the cheese mixture on a floured board. Pat the hard-boiled eggs dry with kitchen paper. Wrap each egg in some of the cheese dough. Press the dough firmly on to the eggs in the palm of the hands until the coating is smooth and free from any cracks. Dip each one in the remaining beaten egg and coat with dry breadcrumbs. Deep-fry in hot oil for 2 minutes until golden brown.

Edam Sausage Pasties

These substantial snacks make an interesting variation on the more usual sausage rolls.

1 × 7½ oz/215 g (½ lb) packet frozen puff pastry, thawed
8 oz/225 g (½ lb) pork sausagemeat
2 sticks celery, grated
1 small cooking apple
4 oz/100 g (1 cup) Edam cheese, grated
salt and pepper
1 egg, beaten

Divide the pastry into four equal portions and roll each into a square approximately 6 inches/15 cm. Trim the edges, using trimmings to make leaves for decoration. Mix together remaining ingredients, reserving a little of the egg for glazing. Divide the filling between each of the pastry squares. Brush the edges with a little beaten egg and make into parcels. Decorate with pastry leaves. Place on a baking sheet and brush with beaten egg. Bake at 220°C/425°F/Gas 7 for 25 minutes or until golden brown.

Ravioli Cheese Snack

Use any kind of hard cheese, but Parmesan, Cheddar or Emmental are probably the best.

Serves 1

1 × 8 oz/225 g (small) can ravioli in tomato sauce
2–3 rashers streaky (Canadian) bacon
2 large slices bread
2 oz/50 g (½ cup) hard cheese, grated

Heat the ravioli through gently in a saucepan. Grill the bacon until crispy. Toast the bread, then sprinkle with the grated cheese and return to the grill to melt and brown the cheese. Put the cheese toasts on to a plate and top with the hot ravioli. Place the grilled bacon on each piece and eat at once.

Sambousek

These Middle Eastern pastries are rather similar to the Indian Samosas. Serve hot or cold.

Pastry
8 oz/225 g (1⅓ cup) flour
2 fl. oz/50 ml (¼ cup) olive oil
1 oz/25 g (3 tbsp) butter, melted
2 fl. oz/50 ml (¼ cup) milk

Filling
7 oz/200 g (2 cups) Feta cheese, crumbled
2 tablespoons freshly chopped parsley
2 teaspoons freshly chopped dill or ½ teaspoon dried dill

To make the pastry, sift the flour into a bowl and make a well in the centre. Pour in the oil, butter and milk and mix with hands to make a soft slightly greasy ball. Place on a floured surface and roll out thinly. Cut into 3 inch/7.5 cm rounds.

To make the filling, break up the cheese with a fork and mix with parsley and dill. Place teaspoonfuls on to the pastry rounds. Brush a little water round the outside of each pastry circle and fold over. Pinch the edges together very firmly and arrange on a greased baking tray. Brush with a little milk. Bake at 180°C/350°F/Gas 4 for 40 minutes until golden brown and risen.

Fried Cheese or Saganaki

A tasty Greek appetizer to serve with ouzo or wine. Several cheeses can be used: Greek Feta or Kefalotiri – the Greek equivalent of Parmesan – or Gruyère or Parmesan. Halloumi cheese can also be used. This will not bubble and should only be fried for 1 minute or it will be too tough.

8 oz/225 g (½ lb) cheese
1 tablespoon flour
2 oz/50 g (¼ cup) butter
juice of ½ lemon
ground black pepper

Cut the cheese into thin slices and coat with flour. Shake off any excess. Melt butter in a small frying pan and, when bubbling, add cheese. Fry for 3–4 minutes, turning once, until melted and bubbling. Sprinkle with lemon juice and freshly ground black pepper.

the flavourings straight into the uncooked case but the finished flan is more likely to have a slightly soggy base.)

Mix the beaten eggs with the cheese, chosen liquid and seasoning, and pour over the top of the flavourings. Add a little more milk if the egg mixture doesn't quite cover the flavourings. Fork it in taking care not to break into the pastry base. Return to the oven and bake for 40–45 minutes until the quiche is lightly browned and set in the centre. Serve hot or cold.

Sale

This classic cheese tart from Switzerland originally used Gruyère but it can be made with any kind of firm cheese. I have tried it very successfully with Double Gloucester and with Leicester. The latter makes a colourful tart.

6 oz/175 g shortcrust pastry
$\frac{1}{2}$ pint/300 ml (1$\frac{1}{4}$ cups) milk
1 small onion, sliced
1 small carrot, sliced
6 peppercorns
1 bay leaf
1 oz/25 g (1$\frac{1}{2}$ tbsp) butter
1 oz/25 g (2 tbsp) flour
salt and pepper
2 tablespoons (3 tbsp) double (heavy) cream
3 eggs, beaten
4 oz/100 g (1 cup) firm cheese, grated
grated nutmeg

Roll out the pastry and use to line an 8 inch/20 cm flan tin. Prick the base all over and bake blind at 190°C/375°F/Gas 5 (with beans and greaseproof or foil) for 20 minutes. Meanwhile heat the milk in a saucepan with the onion, carrot, peppercorns and bay leaf. Cover the pan and infuse for 10 minutes but do not allow the milk to boil. Strain the milk into a basin and clean the pan. Melt the butter in the pan and stir in the flour. Add the strained milk gradually and bring to the boil, stirring all the time. Season and cook for 1 minute. Remove from the heat and beat in the remaining ingredients. Reduce oven heat to 180°C/350°F/Gas 4 and pour filling into the partially cooked pastry case and bake for a further 20–25 minutes. Serve hot.

Swiss Cheese Soufflé Flan

This fluffy flan comes from the Lucerne region of Switzerland. It tends to flop after it comes out of the oven, so serve it at once.

6 oz/175 g shortcrust pastry
4 oz/100 g (1 cup) firm cheese, grated
½ teaspoon mixed dried herbs
2 eggs, separated
¼ pint/150 ml (⅔ cup) single (light) cream
2 fl. oz/50 ml (¼ cup) milk
salt and pepper

Roll out the pastry and use to line an 8 inch/20 cm flan tin. Sprinkle base with cheese and herbs. Mix the egg yolks with the cream and milk and season. Whisk the egg whites until they are really stiff. Mix a tablespoonful of the whites into the yolk and cream mixture and then carefully fold in the rest. Pour the mixture into the flan case and bake at 190°C/375°F/Gas 5 for 15 minutes. Reduce heat to 180°C/350°F/Gas 4 and bake for 15 minutes until golden brown and set in the centre.

Cheese and Pecan Custard Tart

This American recipe uses Colby or Monterey cheese but it also works well with Cheddar or Dunlop cheese.

7 oz/200 g (½ lb) shortcrust pastry
3 oz/75 g (¾ cup) pecans, chopped
4 oz/100 g (1 cup) firm cheese, grated
1 tablespoon cornflour (cornstarch)
8 fl. oz/225 ml (1 cup) milk
4 eggs, beaten

Roll out the pastry and use to line a 9 inch/23 cm flan tin. Prick the base all over. Bake blind for 15 minutes at 180°C/350°F/Gas 4 (with beans, greaseproof paper or foil). Remove from the oven and sprinkle the base with the nuts and cheese. Mix the cornflour with a little of the milk. Stir in the remaining milk and then beat in the four eggs. Pour into the flan case and return to the oven. Bake for 30–35 minutes until the custard is set. Serve hot or warm.

Cheese Pastry Cases

This recipe makes a very rich pastry to be served cold with a cold filling. It can be made up into eighteen tartlets or an 8 inch/20 cm flan case. There are a couple of delicious fillings below, but you can use your imagination!

4 oz/100 g ($\frac{2}{3}$ cup) flour
salt
2 oz/50 g ($\frac{1}{4}$ cup) butter
3 oz/75 g ($\frac{3}{4}$ cup) Cheddar cheese, grated
1 egg

Sift flour and salt into a bowl. Rub in the butter and then mix in the cheese. Bind with egg to give a smooth dough. Roll out pastry and cut into $3\frac{1}{2}$ inch/9 cm rounds. Line tartlet tins. Line pastry cases with greaseproof paper and baking beans and bake at 190°C/375°F/Gas 5 for 10 minutes. Remove beans and paper and return to the oven for 2–3 minutes. Proceed as above for a large flan case but cooking for 20 minutes with the beans, and for a further 10 minutes after that.

EGG AND CURRIED MAYONNAISE

Curry 5 tablespoons mayonnaise to taste. Add 4 chopped hard-boiled eggs and 2 tablespoons raisins. Line the flan or tartlets with chopped watercress and top with the curried egg mixture.

TUNA FISH AND CHIVES

Drain 7 oz/198 g can tuna fish and mix with 1 teaspoon tomato purée and 3 tablespoons mayonnaise. Add 2 tablespoons chopped chives or 2 finely chopped celery sticks. Line the flan or tartlets with shredded lettuce and top with the tuna mixture.

MAIN COURSE DISHES

English Fondue

Using hard cheeses such as Cheddar and Double Gloucester is tasty and successful, but the resulting mix does not have quite the same texture as the Swiss stringy cheeses.

½ pint/300 ml (1¼ cups) dry cider
1 teaspoon made English mustard
1 lb/450 g (4 cups) Mature English Cheddar, grated
1 tablespoon cornflour (cornstarch)
2 tablespoons (3 tbsp) sherry
cubes of crusty bread or lightly toasted white bread

Place the cider and mustard together in the fondue pot or saucepan. Heat until bubbling and add the cheese. Stir to melt the cheese. Blend the cornflour with the sherry and stir into the fondue. Cook, stirring for 1–2 minutes, until the mixture is thick. Keep warm and serve with cubes of bread or toast.

French Fondue

Try experimenting on your own with other cheeses and flavours. I have successfully used Calvados in place of brandy with French Gruyère and juniper berries to enhance the flavour of a gin-based fondue.

1 garlic clove
½ pint/300 ml (1¼ cups) white wine
1¼ lb/550 g (5 cups) Gruyère cheese, grated
1 × 2¾ oz/78 g Boursin cheese
1 tablespoon cornflour (cornstarch)
1 tablespoon brandy
cubes of crusty bread or lightly toasted white bread

Cut the garlic clove in half and rub around the inside of the fondue dish or saucepan. Add the wine and heat until bubbling. Add the grated Gruyère. Cut the Boursin into cubes and add to the pan. Stir over a gentle heat until all the cheese melts. Blend the cornflour with brandy and add to the fondue. Cook for 1–2 minutes until the mixture has thickened. Keep warm and serve with cubes of bread or toast.

Swiss Fondue

Fondue is the national dish of Switzerland. It consists of a variety of cheeses melted with a little flour and alcohol. A special fondue set is used to keep the melted cheese warm and long-handled fondue forks are needed for dipping the bread.

The traditional combination of cheeses for a Neuchâtel Fondue is half and half Swiss Gruyère and Swiss Emmental. Of course both these cheeses are now made in many other countries and any of them can be used very successfully.

Serves 6

1 garlic clove
½ pint/300 ml (1¼ cups) white wine
12 oz/350 g (3 cups) Emmental cheese, grated
12 oz/350 g (3 cups) Gruyère cheese, grated
1 tablespoon cornflour (cornstarch)
2 tablespoons (3 tbsp) Kirsch or gin
cubes of crusty bread or lightly toasted white bread

Cut the garlic clove in half and rub around the inside of the fondue dish or saucepan. Add the wine and heat until bubbling. Add the cheeses, and stir over a gentle heat until they melt. Blend the cornflour with the Kirsch or gin and add to the fondue. Cook for 1–2 minutes until the mixture has thickened. Keep warm and serve with cubes of bread or toast. It is a good idea to stir the fondue each time you place the bread in as this keeps it thick and creamy.

Raclette

This dish takes its name from a Swiss cheese which is traditionally used, but is difficult to get elsewhere. The cheese was meant to be eaten round a wood fire. The Raclette cheese is placed in front of the flames and scraped off as soon as it has melted and is eaten immediately. Nowadays restaurants offering Raclette usually serve boiled potatoes with the melted cheese.

Here's a quick way of cheating if you don't have a special raclette set.

1½ lb/675 g small new potatoes
4 oz/100 g (¼ lb) Raclette or Chaumes cheese

Boil or steam the new potatoes in their skins. Drain and use with the skins on, or peel. Place the potatoes in a heatproof flattish dish. Remove the rind from the Raclette and cut into thin slices. Place on top of the potatoes and place under a hot grill. Serve as soon as the cheese melts.

Aubergines Parmigiana

This Italian classic can be served as a starter or as a main course with salad and potatoes.

3 medium aubergines (eggplant), sliced
1 tablespoon salt
3 tablespoons ($\frac{1}{4}$ cup) flour
5 tablespoons (6 tbsp) oil
4 oz/100 g ($\frac{1}{4}$ lb) Mozzarella cheese, sliced
2 oz/50 g ($\frac{1}{2}$ cup) Parmesan cheese, grated

Tomato Sauce
$\frac{1}{2}$ lb/225 g ($1\frac{1}{3}$ cups) onions, peeled and chopped
1 tablespoon oil
2 × 14 oz/400 g cans tomatoes
1 tablespoon tomato purée
$\frac{1}{2}$ teaspoon sugar
$\frac{1}{4}$ teaspoon salt
$\frac{1}{2}$ teaspoon oregano
ground black pepper

First make the tomato sauce. Fry the onions in the oil for 5 minutes until soft, then add all the remaining ingredients. Bring to the boil and simmer gently for 30–35 minutes until a thick sauce is formed.

Meanwhile layer up the sliced aubergines in a bowl, sprinkling in between layers with salt. Allow to stand for 30 minutes, then rinse well under running water and pat dry with kitchen paper. Lightly coat the aubergines with flour and fry lightly in hot oil in batches. Do not add all the oil at once as aubergines have a tendency to soak it up, which will make the finished dish too oily.

Set the oven to 180°C/350°F/Gas 4. In an ovenproof dish layer the aubergines, tomato sauce, sliced Mozzarella and grated Parmesan. Repeat until the various mixtures have been used up, finishing with cheese layers. Bake in the centre of the preheated oven for 40–45 minutes.

Baked Chicory with Ham

This is a classic dish from Belgium. Serve as a lunch or supper dish. Though Gruyère is in the original recipe, almost any kind of cheese can be used.

4 heads chicory
4 slices ham

Sauce
1 oz/25 g (1½ tbsp) butter
1 oz/25 g (1½ tbsp) flour
½ pint/300 ml (1¼ cups) milk
3 oz/75 g (¾ cup) Gruyère cheese, grated
⅛ teaspoon nutmeg
salt and ground black pepper

Set oven to 190°C/375°F/Gas 5. Wipe the chicory and place in a pan of boiling water and boil for 2–3 minutes. Drain the chicory well and wrap each head in a slice of ham. Place in the bottom of an ovenproof dish.

To make the sauce, melt the butter in a saucepan. Add the flour and cook for 1 minute. Gradually add the milk and bring to the boil, stirring, and cook for 1 minute. Add cheese, nutmeg and seasoning. Stir the mixture to melt the cheese and pour over the chicory. Cook in a preheated oven for 40 minutes.

Pizzas

The original Neapolitan pizza was a substantial dish of bread dough spread with tomatoes and Mozzarella cheese. Nowadays pizza may be made with Cheddar or other firm cheeses, but you won't get that lovely stretchy effect from the cheese.

If you have the time to make pizza at home, simply make up your favourite bread dough and leave it to rise for an hour or so. Knock back and roll out and use to line a baking tray, or you can cut it into the traditional rounds. Brush the dough with oil and then with a good thick tomato sauce made from puréed canned tomatoes and tomato purée. Add the flavourings of your choice – mushrooms, ham, seafood, peppers or spicy sausage – and bake for 20–25 minutes in a hot oven. Add Mozzarella cheese cut into slices about 5–6 minutes before the end of the cooking time.

Macaroni Cheese

Though this dish is Italian in origin it has been popular in Britain since Georgian times.

6 oz/175 g (2 cups) elbow or cut macaroni
salt and pepper
butter
2 oz/50 g ($\frac{1}{3}$ cup) flour
1 pint/600 ml (2$\frac{1}{2}$ cups) milk
4 oz/100 g (1 cup) Cheddar or any other firm cheese, grated

Drop the macaroni into a large pan filled with plenty of boiling water. Add some salt and a knob of butter, and boil for 10–12 minutes or as directed on the packet. Drain and dry on kitchen paper.

Meanwhile melt 2 oz/50 g butter in a pan and stir in the flour. Gradually add the milk and bring to the boil, stirring all the time. Season and cook for 2–3 minutes. Mix in the cooked and drained macaroni and three-quarters of the cheese. Pour into a pie dish. Sprinkle with the remaining cheese. Dot with a further 1 oz/25 g butter and finish off under the grill.

Macaroni à l'Italienne

This recipe comes from Francatelli, Queen Victoria's chef.

6 oz/175 g (2 cups) cut or elbow macaroni
salt
butter
1 × 8 oz/225 g can tomatoes
1 tablespoon tomato purée
2 tablespoons (3 tbsp) canned consommé
3 oz/75 g ($\frac{3}{4}$ cup) Parmesan cheese, grated

Drop the macaroni into a large pan filled with plenty of boiling water. Add the salt and a knob of butter and boil for 10–12 minutes or as directed on the packet. Drain and dry on kitchen paper.

Meanwhile, sieve the contents of the can of tomatoes and stir in the tomato purée and consommé. Pour into a pan and bring to the boil. Layer the cooked macaroni in a pie dish with the tomato sauce, sprinkling each layer with a little cheese. Finish with a cheese layer. Dot with a little more butter and put under a hot grill.

Garlic, Basil and Parmesan Pasta Dressing

Rather surprisingly, crumbled Feta cheese can be used very successfully in place of Parmesan in this pasta sauce. When made with Parmesan, the sauce is known as Pesto.

4 oz/100 g (1 cup) Parmesan cheese, grated, or Feta cheese, crumbled
4 garlic cloves, crushed
1 tablespoon freshly chopped basil
5–6 tablespoons ($\frac{1}{2}$ cup) olive oil

If you are using Parmesan, mix with the garlic and basil to form a thick paste. Add the oil a little at a time, beating all the time. You should end up with a thick green cream. However, it really doesn't matter if the mixture separates. If you decide upon Feta cheese, simply beat all the ingredients together with a fork and don't aim for an emulsified cream.

To serve with spaghetti or noodles, cook about 8–12 oz/225–350 g for five people as directed on the packet, drain and turn into a serving bowl. Pour in the sauce and toss well together. Serve at once.

Panhaggarty

This North Country favourite makes a very good supper dish.

1 tablespoon cooking oil
2 lb/900 g potatoes, thinly sliced
1 lb/450 g onions, thinly sliced
8 oz/225 g (2 cups) firm cheese, grated
salt and pepper
4 rashers bacon (optional)

Heat the oil in a frying pan and place a layer of potato in the bottom. Follow with layers of onion and cheese, seasoning as you go. Repeat the layers until all the ingredients have been used up. Top with rashers of bacon if liked. Cover with a lid and cook over a very low heat for an hour or until all the layers are cooked. Brown under a hot grill to finish off.

Cheese and Potato Pie

There are two ways of making this dish. The ingredients are the same but the method and end result are different.

2 onions, sliced
1 oz/25 g (1½ tbsp) butter
1½ lb/675 g potatoes, peeled and sliced
4 oz/100 g (1 cup) Cheddar cheese, grated
salt and pepper
a little milk or water

METHOD 1

Fry the onions in the butter but do not brown. Layer the onions with the potatoes, cheese and seasoning in a pie dish, ending with a cheese layer. Pour on a little milk or water, and bake at 190°C/375°F/Gas 5 for about an hour until the top is crisp and brown.

METHOD 2

Fry the onions in butter but do not brown. Cook the potatoes in lightly salted boiling water until tender. Drain well and mash with a little milk or water. Stir in the onions and cheese and season to taste. Spoon into a pie dish, fork the top and finish off under a hot grill.

Cheese Pudding

The flavour of this simple dish can be changed by adding different cheeses, herbs or spices. Try with summer savory and German mustard or with thyme and a little Worcestershire sauce.

6 slices bread
1½ oz/40 g (2 tbsp) butter, softened
½ teaspoon dry mustard
pinch of grated nutmeg
pinch of cayenne pepper
6 oz/175 g (1½ cups) hard cheese, grated
2 eggs, beaten
1 pint/600 ml (2½ cups) milk
salt

Toast the bread on one side and cut off the crusts. Mix the butter with the mustard, nutmeg and cayenne and use this mixture to butter the bread on the untoasted side. Cut the buttered toast into fingers and layer, toasted side down, with the cheese in a greased pie dish. Mix the eggs and milk and season with salt. Pour over the bread and cheese and leave to stand for 15–20 minutes. Bake at 180°C/350°F/Gas 4 for 30–40 minutes until lightly browned on top and set in the centre.

Gougère

This cheesy choux pastry case can be filled with any kind of creamy or vegetable mixture. Try it with ratatouille or with chicken or plaice in a light sauce.

$\frac{1}{4}$ pint/150 ml ($\frac{2}{3}$ cup) water

2 oz/50 g (3 tbsp) butter

2$\frac{1}{2}$ oz/60 g ($\frac{1}{3}$ cup) flour

pinch of salt

2 eggs

2 oz/50 g ($\frac{1}{2}$ cup) firm cheese, grated

Heat the water and butter in a saucepan until the butter melts and the water comes to the boil. Quickly add all the flour and the salt. Beat the mixture well over a low heat until the paste is moist and leaves the sides of the pan clean. Remove from the heat and beat in the eggs, one at a time. Beat very well after each addition. The mixture should be shiny and fairly stiff. Beat in the cheese and spoon the mixture round the sides of a medium-sized ovenproof entrée dish. Spoon your chosen filling into the centre and bake at 190°C/375°F/Gas 5 for 40–45 minutes. Remove from the oven and serve at once.

Eggs Mornay

The word Mornay in a recipe usually indicates a light cheese sauce. Though these are usually made with Gruyère or Cheddar, almost any kind of cheese can be pressed into service.
Use the same sauce to pour over poached fish or shellfish for Plaice, Haddock, Scampi or Scallops Mornay.

6 eggs

Sauce
1 oz/25 g (1½ tbsp) butter
1 oz/25 g (2 tbsp) flour
¾ pint/450 ml (2 cups) milk
4 oz/100 g (1 cup) Cheddar cheese, grated
¼ teaspoon dry mustard powder
salt and ground black pepper

Place the eggs in a pan of cold water. Slowly bring to the boil and boil gently for 10–12 minutes.

For the sauce, melt the butter in a saucepan, then add the flour and cook for 1 minute. Gradually add the milk and bring to the boil, stirring, and cook for 1 minute. Add cheese, mustard and seasoning to taste. Heat to melt cheese.

Shell eggs and cut in half lengthways. Place eggs on a warmed dish, cut side down, and pour the sauce over the top. Serve at once or quickly flash under the grill.

Scottish Baked Eggs

This is a much more substantial version of Baked Eggs en Cocotte. It makes a good supper dish. Dunlop is traditional, but any hard cheese can be used.

½ oz/15 g (2 tsp) butter
2 oz/50 g (1 cup) white breadcrumbs
2 oz/50 g (½ cup) hard cheese, grated
4 eggs
salt and pepper
¼ pint/150 ml (⅔ cup) double (heavy) cream

Butter the base of a small ovenproof dish. Mix the breadcrumbs with the cheese and sprinkle half the mixture over the bottom of the dish. Break the eggs carefully over the top. Season and sprinkle with the remaining breadcrumbs and cheese. Spoon the cream all over the top and bake at 180°C/350°F/Gas 4 for 20–30 minutes, depending on how well set you like your eggs.

Cheese Soufflé

The best cheese for a soufflé is a mixture of Parmesan and Gruyère, but a mixture of Cheddar and Parmesan, or Cheddar on its own also work well.

3 oz/75 g ($\frac{1}{3}$ cup) butter
2 oz/50 g ($\frac{1}{3}$ cup) flour
$\frac{1}{2}$ pint/300 ml (1$\frac{1}{4}$ cups) milk
4 oz/100 g (1 cup) hard cheese, grated
salt and pepper
$\frac{1}{2}$ teaspoon dry mustard powder (optional)
3 eggs, separated

Melt the butter in a saucepan. Add the flour and cook for a minute or so. Gradually add the milk and bring the mixture to the boil, stirring all the time. Add the cheese, seasoning and mustard if used. Remove from the heat and beat in the egg yolks. Stiffly whisk the egg whites and stir a couple of tablespoons into the mixture. Fold in the rest of the egg whites and spoon the mixture into a greased 2 pint/1.2 litre soufflé dish. Bake at 190°C/375°F/Gas 5 for 45–50 minutes until browned and risen and set in the centre.

Quick Cheese Soufflé

A very light cheese soufflé can be made without first making a roux. However, it flops even more quickly than a regular soufflé once it has been removed from the oven.

Serves 2

3 eggs, separated
4 oz/100 g (1 cup) hard cheese, grated
salt and pepper

Mix the egg yolks, cheese and seasoning. Whisk the egg whites until they are very stiff and fold into the cheese mixture. Spoon into a 1$\frac{1}{2}$ pint/900 ml greased soufflé dish and bake at 190°C/375°F/Gas 5 for about 40 minutes. Serve at once.

Coquilles Fruits De Mer

Serve in individual scallop shells for special occasion meals, or make in a long shallow dish if you are in a hurry.

8 oz/225 g ($\frac{1}{2}$ lb) cod
$\frac{1}{4}$ pint/150 ml ($\frac{2}{3}$ cup) milk
1 bay leaf
6 peppercorns
$\frac{1}{4}$ pint/150 ml ($\frac{2}{3}$ cup) canned condensed crab bisque or soup
4 oz/100 g ($\frac{2}{3}$ cup) peeled prawns (shrimps)
salt and pepper
lemon juice
1 lb/450 g potatoes, boiled
3 oz/75 g ($\frac{3}{4}$ cup) Cheshire cheese, grated
1 oz/25 g ($\frac{1}{2}$ cup) breadcrumbs
lemon and parsley for garnish

Put the cod into a saucepan with the milk, bay leaf and peppercorns. Cover and cook gently until the fish is tender. Remove fish, discard skin and bones and divide the fish into chunks. Strain the liquid and put to one side.

Put the crab bisque into a saucepan, heat through gently, add enough of the fish liquor to make into a coating consistency. Stir in the cod and prawns. Add seasoning and a few drops of lemon juice to taste.

Mash the potato with the remainder of the fish liquor and season to taste. Pipe around the edge of four scallop shells or individual dishes. Spoon the fish mixture into the centre of each. Sprinkle the cheese and breadcrumbs over.

Brown under the grill or in the oven. Serve garnished with lemon and parsley.

Scandinavian Cheesy Fish Cakes

Use Mesost for an authentic flavour, and serve with horseradish sauce.

12 oz/350 g ($\frac{3}{4}$ lb) white fish, skinned and boned (cod, haddock, huss or coley)

2 oz/50 g ($\frac{1}{2}$ cup) Scandinavian whey cheese, grated

1 lb/450 g cooked and mashed potato

4 tablespoons ($\frac{1}{3}$ cup) white or brown breadcrumbs

$\frac{1}{2}$ teaspoon dried dill

salt and pepper

flour

butter for frying

Mince the fish and mix with all the remaining ingredients except the flour and butter. Shape into eight flat fish cakes. Coat with flour and fry in hot butter for about 4–5 minutes on each side until crisp and golden.

White Fish Mornay

This classic dish is made with Emmental and Parmesan, but any hard cheese can be used in place of the Emmental.

1$\frac{1}{2}$ lb/675 g white fish such as cod, haddock or plaice

$\frac{1}{2}$ pint/300 ml (1$\frac{1}{4}$ cups) milk

1 oz/25 g (1$\frac{1}{2}$ tbsp) butter

1 oz/25 g (2 tbsp) flour

1$\frac{1}{2}$ oz/40 g ($\frac{1}{3}$ cup) hard cheese, grated

1$\frac{1}{2}$ oz/40 g ($\frac{1}{3}$ cup) Parmesan cheese, grated

salt and ground black pepper

Set the oven to 190°C/375°F/Gas 5. Skin fish and roll fillets up, or cut into cubes. Place the fish in a lightly greased ovenproof dish, cover with milk and foil, and bake in the preheated oven for 25–30 minutes or until the fish is cooked. Drain off the cooking liquor and make up $\frac{1}{2}$ pint/300 ml with milk. Keep th fish warm.

To make the sauce, melt the butter in a pan. Add the flour and cook for 1 minute. Gradually add the fishy milk and bring to the boil, stirring, and cook for 1 minute. Add cheeses and seasoning to taste. Heat to melt cheese. Poor sauce over the fish and serve immediately.

Sole and Shrimp Pudding

This dish makes a most unusual centrepiece for a dinner party. Serve with a light and creamy roux sauce flavoured with a dash of anchovy essence.

2 small lemon or Dover sole, filleted and skinned
1½ lb/675 g cold cooked, peeled potatoes
5 oz/150 g (1¼ cups) English Farmhouse cheese, grated
1 oz/25 g (1½ tbsp) butter
2 small eggs
salt and pepper
6 oz/175 g (1 cup) peeled prawns (shrimps)
3 tablespoons (¼ cup) chopped parsley
sprigs of parsley to garnish

Butter a 1¾ pint/1 litre pudding basin and line with the sole fillets. Mash the potatoes with the cheese, butter and eggs, and season to taste. Fill the centre of the pudding basin with alternate layers of the potato mixture and prawns mixed with parsley. Cover with greased foil and place in a roasting tin filled with 1 inch/2.5 cm hot water. Bake at 180°C/350°F/Gas 4 for 30–35 minutes. Leave to stand for 5 minutes and then turn out. Decorate with sprigs of parsley and serve at once.

Scottish Fish Pie

This creamy pie has a crumbly cheese-flavoured topping which could be used on a variety of dishes. Use Dunlop cheese for a traditional flavour.

1 lb/450 g Finnan haddock, filleted
½ pint/300 ml (1¼ cups) milk
3 oz/75 g (⅓ cup) butter
1 onion, finely chopped
3 oz/75 g (½ cup) flour
1 teaspoon lemon juice
2 softly boiled eggs, chopped
salt and pepper
¼ teaspoon dry mustard
2 oz/50 g (½ cup) hard cheese, finely grated

Right: *Gruyère Moons (page 33).*

Overleaf: *'Just As You Like It' Cheese Quiche (page) 48, Coquilles Fruits de Mer (page 62).*

Poach the haddock in the milk for 5–6 minutes. Remove the fish and flake it. Strain the milk and keep on one side. Melt half the butter in a pan and gently fry the onion in this until it softens. Stir in half the flour and cook for a minute or so. Stir in the flavoured milk and bring to the boil, stirring all the time. Stir in the lemon juice, egg and fish and season to taste. Spoon the mixture into an ovenproof dish. Rub the remaining butter into the remaining flour and stir in the mustard and cheese and sprinkle over the top. Bake at 200°C/400°F/Gas 6 for 20 minutes.

Stuffed Fish Fillets

Almost any kind of hard or semi-hard cheese can be used in this dish. You could also use blue cheese but this can be rather a strong flavour with fish, so use half and half blue cheese and plain cheese.

8 fillets of fish from 4 small whiting, or 2 plaice or lemon sole, skinned
black pepper
1 egg, beaten
2 oz/50 g (1 cup) fresh breadcrumbs
2 oz/50 g ($\frac{1}{4}$ cup) butter, melted
1 teaspoon paprika pepper

Stuffing
6 oz/175 g (1$\frac{1}{2}$ cups) cheese, grated
3 oz/75 g (1$\frac{1}{2}$ cups) breadcrumbs
1 egg
black pepper

Wipe the fish fillets with a damp cloth and sprinkle all over with pepper. Mix all the stuffing ingredients together and place a spoonful on each fish fillet. Roll the fillets up and dip each one in beaten egg and then in breadcrumbs. Place on an ovenproof dish and pour the melted butter over the top. Sprinkle with paprika. Bake at 180°C/350°F/Gas 4 for 25–30 minutes until the fish is cooked through.

Left: *Cheesy Vegetable Pie (page 73).*

Devilled Crab

Devilled is an English culinary expression. It usually means that mustard and Worcestershire sauce have been included in the recipe.

2½–3 lb/1.1–1.4 kg dressed crab
 or ¾ lb/350 g crab meat
2 oz/50 g (¼ cup) butter
4 oz/100 g (⅔ cup) onions, peeled and finely chopped
5 tablespoons (6 tbsp) double (heavy) cream
2 teaspoons English made mustard
1 teaspoon Worcestershire sauce
3 dashes Tabasco sauce
good pinch of cayenne pepper
2 oz/50 g (1 cup) white breadcrumbs
2 tablespoons (3 tbsp) freshly grated Parmesan cheese

Topping
1 tablespoon freshly grated Parmesan cheese
1 tablespoon white breadcrumbs

Remove the light and the dark meat from the crab. Melt the butter and fry the onion for 5 minutes until soft. Set the oven to 200°C/400°F/Gas 6. Mix crab meat with softened onion, cream, mustard, Worcestershire sauce, Tabasco, cayenne, breadcrumbs and Parmesan cheese. Stir well and return to crab shell. This is quite a tight fit, so you may prefer to put the mixture into an ovenproof dish. Mix topping together and sprinkle over crab. Bake in the preheated oven for 20 minutes and serve with a salad.

Lobster Thermidor

Have the lobsters cleaned and split in half lengthways by the fishmonger.

2 cooked lobsters, weighing 1–1¼ lb (450–550 g) each

Sauce
8 fl. oz/225 ml (1 cup) milk
1 bay leaf
1 small onion, peeled and quartered
4 peppercorns
3 oz/75 g (⅓ cup) butter
1 oz/25 g (2 tbsp) flour
1 oz/25 g (2 tbsp) white wine
1 teaspoon French Dijon mustard
2 tablespoons (3 tbsp) double (heavy) cream
salt and pepper
2 oz/50 g (1 cup) browned breadcrumbs
3 tablespoons (4 tbsp) grated Parmesan cheese

Heat the milk with the bay leaf, onion and peppercorns, then remove from the heat and allow to infuse for 10 minutes. Set the oven to 200°C/400°F/Gas 6. Remove the flesh from the body and claws of the lobster and cut into ½ inch/1.25 cm cubes. Heat 2 oz/50 g of the butter in a saucepan, add lobster cubes and fry for 3–4 minutes, turning frequently. Return lobster meat to shells and place in ovenproof dish.

Add the remaining butter to the pan, stir in the flour and cook for 1 minute. Strain the milk and gradually add to the pan with the wine. Bring the sauce to the boil, stirring, and cook for 1 minute. Add mustard and cream to sauce, adjust seasoning and pour over lobster in shells.

Mix together the breadcrumbs and grated Parmesan cheese and sprinkle over lobster. Heat through in a pre-heated oven for 15 minutes or until golden brown and bubbling.

67

Huntingdon Scallops

The ham, cheese and breadcrumb coating in the recipe can also be used to good effect with small pieces of white fish, chicken or florets of cauliflower or broccoli.

1 tablespoon olive oil
juice of $\frac{1}{2}$ lemon
1 teaspoon freshly chopped parsley
salt and pepper
8 scallops, sliced
fat for deep-frying

Coating
4 oz/100 g ($\frac{2}{3}$ cup) cooked ham, minced
4 oz/100 g (2 cups) fresh white breadcrumbs
1 oz/25 g ($\frac{1}{4}$ cup) Parmesan cheese, grated
4 spring onions (scallions) or 2 shallots, very finely chopped
seasoned flour
2 eggs, beaten

Mix the olive oil, lemon juice, parsley and seasoning and pour over the scallops. Leave to stand for 30 minutes. Meanwhile mix together the ham, breadcrumbs, cheese and chopped onion. Drain the scallops and dry on kitchen paper. Dip in seasoned flour and then in beaten egg. Coat with the ham and breadcrumb mixture, pressing it firmly down on to the fish. Fry in hot deep fat until crisp and brown.

Chicken Cordon Bleu

This well-known dish is easier to make than you might think. Any kind of cheese can be placed in the stuffing, although Gruyère is classic.

4 large chicken breasts, skinned and boned
4 oz/100 g firm cheese
2 slices ham
1 egg, beaten
3 oz/75 g (1$\frac{1}{2}$ cups) breadcrumbs
oil for deep-frying

Make a cut horizontally through the centre of each chicken breast to form a deep pocket. Slice cheese into four equal-sized pieces. Cut ham slices in half and wrap half a slice of ham around each piece of cheese. Insert one of these ham rolls into the pocket of each chicken breast. If you wish, secure the slit with a cocktail stick.

Dip each chicken breast in beaten egg and then coat in breadcrumbs. Chill until required. Deep-fry the chicken parcels in hot oil for about 12–15 minutes until the coating is golden brown and chicken is cooked.

Italian Bocconcini

The name of this Italian classic literally means little mouthfuls and delicious they are too. Almost any kind of stringy cheese can be used, but Gruyère is usual.

Another classic italian dish called Saltimbocca can be made by substituting a sage leaf for each piece of cheese and following the same method.

4–5 veal escalopes
4–5 slices Prosciutto ham
4 oz/100 g firm cheese
2 oz/50 g ($\frac{1}{4}$ cup) butter
3 fl. oz/75 ml (6 tbsp) Marsala wine
2 tablespoons (3 tbsp) freshly chopped parsley (optional)

Place the escalopes between pieces of greaseproof paper and beat until thin. Cut the flattened escalopes into four slices and cut a piece of Prosciutto to fit each. Cut cheese into sixteen to twenty equal-sized pieces and place one in the centre of the Prosciutto. Roll up the meat and secure each roll with a wooden cocktail stick. Repeat until all the mixture is used up.

Melt butter in a frying pan and fry the little packets of veal for 5 minutes, turning to brown on all sides. Pour in the Marsala, cover, and simmer for 4–5 minutes. Sprinkle with parsley, if used, and serve immediately with the Marsala sauce.

Veal Cordon Bleu

This French classic makes an excellent dinner-party dish. It can be prepared up to the breadcrumb stage well in advance.

4 × 4 oz/100 g veal escalopes

4 small slices ham

4 oz/100 g Gruyère cheese

2 tablespoons (3 tbsp) flour

pinch of salt

ground black pepper

1 egg, beaten

4 oz/100 g (2 cups) white breadcrumbs

oil for frying

Place each escalope between two sheets of greaseproof paper and beat, using a rolling pin, until flattened and doubled in size. Place a slice of ham on one side of the top of each escalope. Slice the cheese thinly and place on top of the ham. Fold over the other half of the escalope to form a sandwich.

Mix flour, salt and pepper together and lightly coat each escalope. Dip in beaten egg and then in breadcrumbs. Shallow-fry in ¼ inch/6 mm oil for 3–4 minutes on each side until golden. Drain on absorbent paper and serve.

Cheesy Lamb Hotpot

This dish can be a little fatty but if you cut all the excess fat off the lamb, the end result is just about acceptable. However, it's so delicious you'll want to make it more often than perhaps you should!

4 large lamb chops, all fat removed

salt and pepper

2 onions, sliced

1 tablespoon cooking oil

1 lb/450 g potatoes, peeled and cut into chunks

3 fl. oz/75 ml (6 tbsp) water

4 tomatoes, peeled and sliced

4 oz/100 g (1 cup) firm cheese, grated

Season the chops and place in the base of a casserole or hotpot dish. Gently fry the onions in the oil to soften. When they turn transparent, mix with the potatoes and spoon over the chops. Next pour in the water. Finally add a layer of tomatoes and a layer of cheese. Cover and bake at 180°C/350°F/Gas 4 for 1 hour. Remove the lid and continue cooking for a further 15–20 minutes to brown the cheese.

ACCOMPANIMENTS AND SALADS

Cauliflower and Fennel au Gratin

This is an interesting variation on the straightforward Cauliflower au Gratin. If you prefer the original, simply leave out the fennel and buy a larger cauliflower.

½ pint/300 ml (1¼ cups) water
1 small cauliflower
2 heads fennel, coarsely chopped
milk
2 oz/50 g (¼ cup) butter
2 oz/50 g (⅓ cup) flour
3 oz/75 g (¾ cup) cheese, grated
salt and pepper

Pour the water into a large pan and add the whole cauliflower and the chopped fennel. Bring to the boil and simmer for 15 minutes until the vegetables are just tender. Do not allow the vegetables to over-cook or they will go mushy. Drain off the cooking liquor and make up to 1 pint/600 ml with milk. Cut the cauliflower into pieces and arrange in a large shallow casserole with the fennel. Keep warm.

Melt the butter in a pan, add the flour, and stir well. Gradually add the milk and cauliflower water, stirring all the time. Bring to the boil and cook for 2–3 minutes. Add three-quarters of the cheese and season to taste. Pour over the cauliflower and fennel and top with remaining cheese. Place under a hot grill to brown, and serve at once.

Cauliflower and Potato Gratin

This is a much quicker way of making a gratin dish in that you do not need to make a roux or flour-based sauce. This recipe makes a very good vegetarian main course dish. Use Gruyère, Emmental or Cheddar.

2 lb/900 g potatoes, peeled and sliced
salt
½ pint/300 ml (1¼ cups) milk
1 large cauliflower, cut into large florets
6 oz/175 g (1½ cups) firm cheese, grated
½ pint/300 ml (1¼ cups) single (light) cream
black pepper
grated nutmeg

Set the oven to 200°C/400°F/Gas 6. Place the potatoes in a saucepan with salt and milk, and add sufficient water to just cover the potatoes. Arrange the cauliflower florets on the top. Cover and bring to the boil. Simmer for 10 minutes. Remove the cauliflower and keep on one side. Spoon out the potato and arrange half in the centre of a shallow ovenproof dish. Arrange the cauliflower around the outside. Sprinkle with half the cheese. Pile the rest of the potatoes into the centre. Sprinkle with the remaining cheese and pour on the cream and 6–7 tablespoons of the cooking liquid. Sprinkle with pepper and nutmeg and finish off for about 20–30 minutes in the oven.

Celery Cheese

Any kind of English Farmhouse cheese can be used in this recipe. However, the original – which comes from Northumberland – used Cheddar.

1 head celery
black pepper
½ pint/300 ml (1¼ cups) milk
3 oz/75 g (¾ cup) firm cheese, grated
1 egg, beaten
1 oz/25 g (½ cup) fresh breadcrumbs

Clean the celery and chop the sticks very finely. Place in a saucepan with the pepper and barely cover with milk. Bring gently to the boil and simmer uncovered for about 15 minutes until tender, stirring occasionally. Leave to cool and then mix in the cheese and beaten egg. Spoon into a greased pie dish. Sprinkle the bread-crumbs over the top and bake at 180°C/350°F/Gas 4 for 30 minutes until lightly browned.

Cheesy Vegetable Pie

Use any vegetables in season, or take the easy way out with frozen mixed vegetables.

Serves 6

1½ lb/675 g boiled potatoes, drained and mashed
2 oz/50 g (¼ cup) butter
1 egg, beaten
2 lb/900 g cooked, sliced vegetables (carrots, onions, celery)

Sauce
2 oz/50 g (¼ cup) butter
2 oz/50 g (⅓ cup) flour
1 pint/600 ml (2½ cups) milk
4 oz/100 g (1 cup) Cheddar cheese, finely grated
salt and pepper
1 teaspoon chopped parsley to garnish

Sieve the mashed potato and beat in the butter and egg thoroughly until smooth. Using a large star pipe, pipe the potato around the edge of the dish to form a deep crust. Brown under the grill or in a hot oven for 15–20 minutes.

To prepare the sauce, melt the butter, add the flour and cook over a low heat for a few minutes. Gradually blend in the milk and cook, stirring continuously, until the sauce boils and thickens. Stir in the cheese and sea-son with a little salt and pepper.

Arrange the vegetables and sauce in layers in the centre of the dish, finishing with the sauce. Sprinkle with chopped parsley and serve immediately.

Courgettes Provençal

All kinds of other vegetables can be treated in this way. Alternatively they can be mixed with the courgettes. Try adding potatoes or aubergines for a more substantial dish. Use any hard cheese.

1 large onion, sliced
1 garlic clove, crushed (optional)
knob of butter
1 lb/450 g courgettes (zucchini), sliced
4 oz/100 g (1 cup) hard cheese, grated
4 tomatoes, peeled, seeded and chopped
1 tablespoon tomato purée
$\frac{1}{2}$ teaspoon dried thyme
pinch of dried rosemary
pinch of fennel seeds
salt and pepper

Gently fry the onion and garlic, if used, in the butter. When softened, layer in a heatproof dish with the courgettes and cheese. Mix the tomato and tomato purée with 2 tablespoons of water and all the herbs and seasonings. Pour the mixture over the vegetables. Cover with a lid and bake at 190°C/375°F/Gas 5 for about 40 minutes.

French Cheesy Potatoes or Potato Gratin

Cheese and potatoes go very well together. Here's a baked potato dish from France which usually uses Gruyère or Emmental. However almost any hard or semi-hard cheese can be used. It's very good, too, made with a little blue cheese mixed into the plain cheese.

1$\frac{1}{2}$ lb/675 g potatoes, peeled and sliced
1 pint/600 ml (2$\frac{1}{2}$ cups) milk
$\frac{1}{4}$ pint/150 ml ($\frac{2}{3}$ cup) double (heavy) cream
3 oz/75 g ($\frac{3}{4}$ cup) cheese, grated
salt and pepper

Put the potatoes and milk in a pan and bring to the boil. Cook over a very low heat for 10 minutes. Transfer the potatoes to a shallow heatproof dish. Pour in sufficient of the cooking liquor to come about half-way up the potatoes. Pour on the cream and sprinkle with cheese and seasoning. Bake at 200°C/400°F/Gas 6 for about 20–30 minutes until browned.

Hasselback Potatoes

Try this unusual Swedish recipe for baked potatoes for a change. The traditional way is to peel the potatoes but they are very good with their skins on too.

12 small to medium potatoes
3 tablespoons ($\frac{1}{4}$ cup) melted butter
1 tablespoon dry breadcrumbs
4 tablespoons ($\frac{1}{3}$ cup) hard cheese, grated
salt and pepper

Peel the potatoes or leave in their (well scrubbed) jackets. Cut a slice off one side so that they will sit flat on a greased baking tray. Make vertical slices into the potato at $\frac{1}{8}$ inch/3 mm intervals. Do not slice all the way through: it is important that the potatoes should remain joined at the base. Pour half the butter over the potatoes and bake at 220°C/425°F/Gas 7 for 30 minutes. Baste with the butter from time to time. After 30 minutes sprinkle the potatoes with breadcrumbs, cheese and seasoning and pour on any remaining butter. Bake for a further 15 minutes or until the potatoes feel soft when tested with a tooth pick.

Bogota Rice

This way of cooking rice is typical of many Latin-American dishes with a Spanish influence. Serve with chicken casseroles. Use Cheddar or any other hard cheese.

5 oz/150 g ($\frac{2}{3}$ cup) long-grain rice
salt
$\frac{1}{2}$ pint/300 ml (1$\frac{1}{4}$ cups) water
1 oz/25 g (1$\frac{1}{2}$ tbsp) butter
2 oz/50 g ($\frac{1}{2}$ cup) hard cheese, grated
2 teaspoons sugar
2 eggs, beaten

Drop the rice into the boiling salted water, stir and cover with a lid. Reduce the heat and cook for 12–15 minutes until the rice is tender and all the liquid has been taken up. Mix the drained rice with all the remaining ingredients and pour into a heatproof pudding basin or small casserole. Stand the basin in 1 inch/2.5 cm hot water in a roasting tin and bake at 180°C/350°F/Gas 4 for 40 minutes until set. Serve at once.

Parmesan Dumplings

These dumplings are very good in clear soup, or they can be served with roast meats or casseroles.

6 oz/175 g (3 cups) breadcrumbs
4 tablespoons (⅓ cup) grated Parmesan cheese
2 oz/50 g (⅓ cup) finely chopped onion
1 oz/25 g (2 tbsp) flour
ground black pepper

Mix together the breadcrumbs, Parmesan cheese, chopped onion, flour and pepper. Mix well to form a dough, then divide in eight equal balls using floured hands. Make more smaller balls if going into the soup. Cook the dumplings by gently poaching them in well flavoured stock or soup for 20 minutes.

Smoky Cheese and Potato Salad

Any of the smoked cheeses currently available can be used in this simple salad recipe.

1 lb/450 g new potatoes, scrubbed
4 oz/100 g (1½ cups) smoked cheese, cut into small cubes
2 spring onions (scallions), finely chopped
1 green apple, cored and cut into small cubes
4 tablespoons (⅓ cup) soured cream or yogurt
salt and pepper

Cook the new potatoes in their skins. Chop, or peel and chop, while they are still hot. Leave to cool a little and then mix with the cheese and spring onion. When the mixture is completely cold stir in all the remaining ingredients.

Curly Endive and Smoked Cheese Salad

This salad can be made with any firm cheese, but smoked cheese really does have the edge!

½ head curly endive
2 slices white bread, crusts removed
1 garlic clove
2 oz/50 g (¼ cup) butter
3 oz/75 g (1 cup) smoked cheese, cut into sticks
4 tablespoons (⅓ cup) vinaigrette dressing

Soak the curly endive in cold water. Remove any shrivelled pieces and drain well. Rub the bread with the cut clove of garlic and then cut into small cubes. Fry these cubes in hot butter until golden brown. Toss the curly endive with the smoked cheese sticks and garlic bread croûtons. Pour on the dressing and serve at once.

Chef's Salad

The semi-hard slicing cheeses such as Gouda, Samsø or Tilsit are particularly suited to this recipe. Smoked cheese can be used to give a change of flavour.

2 slices each of ham and tongue, or 4 slices ham
6 oz/175 g cheese, cut into slices
1 green pepper, seeded and thinly sliced
2 carrots, coarsely grated
lettuce leaves
½ bunch watercress, cut into sprigs
4 tablespoons (⅓ cup) vinaigrette or French dressing

Cut the ham, tongue if used, and the cheese into thin strips and mix with the pepper and carrots. Arrange the lettuce leaves on a serving plate and pile the shredded mixture in the centre. Surround with sprigs of watercress. Spoon the dressing over the top of the salad and serve.

77

Cheese Log

*Any kind of English Farmhouse
cheese works well in this recipe. I
particularly like Red Leicester or
Lancashire.*

8 oz/225 g (2 cups) English Farmhouse cheese, grated
8 oz/225 g (2 cups) carrots, grated
1 sweet-sour cucumber, finely chopped
1 tablespoon freshly chopped parsley
2 tablespoons (3 tbsp) mayonnaise
salt and pepper
single (light) cream or milk

Mix all the ingredients together, adding sufficient cream
or milk to give a moist texture. Shape the mixture into
a roll or press into a loaf tin. If shaping into a roll,
wrap in foil. Chill for 2–3 hours. Unwrap or turn out
and serve cut into slices.

DESSERTS AND BAKING

Apple and Wensleydale Pie

*This is a traditional way of making
apple pie in Yorkshire.*

Pastry
8 oz/225 g ($1\frac{1}{3}$ cups) flour
pinch of salt
2 oz/50 g ($\frac{1}{4}$ cup) butter
2 oz/50 g ($\frac{1}{4}$ cup) lard
water

Filling
$1\frac{1}{4}$ lb/550 g cooking apples
3 oz/75 g ($\frac{1}{3}$ cup) sugar
1 teaspoon cornflour (cornstarch)
4 oz/100 g Wensleydale cheese

Set the oven to 200°C/400°F/Gas 6. To make the pastry,
sift the flour and salt into a bowl. Rub in the butter
and lard until the mixture resembles fine breadcrumbs
and then add enough water to give a soft, non-sticky

dough. Wrap in clingfilm and chill.

To make the filling, peel, core and slice the cooking apples. Cut cheese into ½ inch/1.25 cm cubes. Mix the sugar with the cornflour and add to the cheese.

Roll out half the pastry and line an 8 inch/20 cm pie plate. Fill pie by layering up apples, cheese and sugar. Roll out remaining pastry, dampen edges of pie rim and place lid on top. Trim edges and decorate. Bake in the preheated oven for 30–35 minutes.

Cheese Bread

I like this recipe made with Lancashire cheese, but any kind of firm cheese can be used.

6 fl. oz/175 ml (¾ cup) semi-skimmed milk

½ oz/15 g (2 tsp) butter

6 oz/175 g (1 cup) wholemeal flour

7 oz/200 g (1¼ cups) rye flour

½ teaspoon salt

½ sachet or 3 teaspoons (1 tbsp) Easybake yeast

½ teaspoon paprika pepper

pinch of cayenne pepper

pinch of dried thyme

2 oz/50 g (½ cup) hard cheese, grated

1 egg, beaten

Heat the milk in a pan and melt the butter in it. Do not allow the mixture to boil. Place the flours, salt, yeast, paprika, cayenne, thyme and cheese in a bowl. Beat the egg into the lukewarm milk and make up to ½ pint/300 ml with lukewarm water. Make a well in the centre of the dry ingredients and pour in the liquid. Mix to a dough. Place on a floured surface and knead for 10 minutes until elastic. Place in a 1 lb/450 g loaf tin and leave in a warm place to rise (1–1½ hours). Bake at 220°C/425°F/Gas 7 for 20 minutes. Reduce heat to 190°C/375°F/Gas 5 and bake for a further 30 minutes until cooked.

Russian Cheese Bread

This recipe comes from the Georgian area of the Southern USSR. I used Caerphilly very successfully but any crumbly cheese could be used.

12 oz/350 g (2 cups) flour

½ teaspoon salt

½ sachet or 3 teaspoons Easybake yeast

2 oz/50 g (¼ cup) butter, melted

7 fl. oz/200 ml (⅞ cup) lukewarm water

Filling

1 lb/450 g (5⅓ cups) cheese, crumbled

1 egg

1 oz/25 g butter (1½ tbsp), softened

1 tablespoon freshly chopped parsley

salt and pepper

Place the dry ingredients in a bowl and make a well in the centre. Mix the butter and sufficient lukewarm water to make a good dough and pour into the well. Mix to a dough. Turn on to a floured surface and knead for 10 minutes until elastic. Place in a bowl covered with clingfilm and leave in a warm place to rise for 45 minutes.

Meanwhile mix all the filling ingredients together. Roll out the risen dough thickly and use to line a greased 8 inch/20 cm loose-based cake tin, leaving the dough flapping over the sides. Spoon filling into the centre and then gather up the edges of the dough and fold over the top. Pinch the centre together. Leave to rise again for 20–30 minutes. Bake at 200°C/400°F/Gas 6 for 30 minutes. Reduce the heat to 180°C/350°F/Gas 4 and continue baking for a further 30 minutes until the bread is deep golden in colour. Leave to cool in the tin for 15 minutes. Eat while still warm.

Cheesy Picnic Loaf

This makes a filling snack or just a good loaf to take on picnics. I also cut it into small chunks and serve with drinks. Use Tilsit or any semi-hard cheese.

½ red pepper, seeded and finely chopped
½ green pepper, seeded and finely chopped
1 small onion, finely chopped
3 oz/75 g (⅓ cup) butter
4 oz/100 g (⅔ cup) self-raising flour
6 oz/175 g (1½ cup) semi-hard cheese, grated
2 oz/50 g (⅓ cup) salami or smoked ham, finely chopped
3 eggs, beaten
salt and freshly ground black pepper
pinch of celery salt (optional)

Gently fry the peppers and onion for 3–4 minutes in the butter to soften them. Place in a bowl, sift in the flour, and add all the remaining ingredients. Mix well together and spoon into a greased 1½ lb/675 g loaf tin. Bake at 190°C/375°F/Gas 5 for 50 minutes. Loosen the sides with a palette knife and leave to cool in the tin. Turn out and cut into slices or chunks to serve.

Cheese and Apple Loaf

This recipe makes a deliciously moist loaf which slices well.

4 oz/100 g (½ cup) butter
6 oz/175 g (¾ cup) caster sugar
2 eggs
8 oz/225 g (1 cup) unpeeled eating apples, cored and grated
4 oz/100 g (1 cup) Cheddar cheese, grated
2 oz/50 g (½ cup) walnuts, chopped
1 lb/450 g (2⅔ cups) flour
½ oz/15 g (1 scant tbsp) baking powder
½ teaspoon bicarbonate of soda
½ teaspoon salt
4 tablespoons (⅓ cup) milk

Cream the butter and sugar and then beat in the eggs, apples, cheese and nuts. Stir in the flour, baking powder, bicarbonate of soda, salt and milk. Line and grease a 2 lb/900 g loaf tin. Spoon the mixture into the tin and bake at 180°C/350°F/Gas 4 for 1½ hours. Turn out to cool on a wire rack.

Italian Mozzarella Bread

Serve this delicious variant on garlic bread with a plain grilled steak or with roast lamb.

1 small rye and caraway seed loaf or a Vienna loaf

2 oz/50 g ($\frac{1}{4}$ cup) butter, softened

6 oz/175 g ($1\frac{1}{2}$ cups) Mozzarella cheese, grated

$\frac{1}{2}$ teaspoon dried oregano

$\frac{1}{4}$ teaspoon dried basil

1 × $1\frac{3}{4}$ oz/50 g can anchovies, washed and drained

Slice the loaf at $\frac{1}{2}$ inch/1.25 cm intervals, almost but not quite through to the base. Mix the butter and Mozzarella and spread a little of the mixture between each slice of bread. Spread the tops of the loaf with a little more butter and sprinkle with herbs. Place the anchovies in a criss-cross pattern over the top of the bread. Place the loaf on a greased baking tray and bake at 220°C/425°F/Gas 7 for 10–15 minutes. Serve at once.

Cheese Scones

For a change, use best mild beer in place of milk and add 4 rashers of streaky bacon which have been grilled and chopped.

Makes 10–12

8 oz/225 g ($1\frac{1}{3}$ cups) flour

$\frac{1}{2}$ teaspoon salt

$2\frac{1}{2}$ teaspoons (1 tbsp) baking powder

$\frac{1}{2}$ teaspoon dry mustard powder

2 oz/50 g ($\frac{1}{4}$ cup) butter

4 oz/100 g (1 cup) mature Cheddar cheese, grated

$\frac{1}{4}$ pint/150 ml ($\frac{2}{3}$ cup) milk

Sieve the flour, salt, baking powder and mustard into a bowl. Rub in the butter until the mixture resembles fine breadcrumbs. Stir in the grated cheese and mix in the milk to give a smooth dough. Knead the scone mixture lightly and roll out on a lightly floured surface 2 inches/5 cm in thickness. Cut into $2\frac{1}{2}$ inch/6.5 cm rounds and bake at 220°C/425°F/Gas 7 and 10–12 minutes or until scones are golden brown.

Dutch Cheese Biscuits

Serve with cheese, or sandwich biscuits together with a creamy filling such as cream cheese and prawns and serve as a light snack. These biscuits are best made with slightly waxy cheese like Edam, Gouda or Tilsit. With cheeses such as Cheddar or Gloucester you may need to add a little more flour.

Makes 16–18

4 oz/100 g ($\frac{2}{3}$ cup) flour
1 teaspoon dry mustard powder
pinch of salt
2 oz/50 g ($\frac{1}{4}$ cup) margarine
2 oz/50 g ($\frac{1}{2}$ cup) cheese, grated
2–2$\frac{1}{2}$ tablespoons (3 tbsp) water

Topping
1 egg
$\frac{1}{2}$ teaspoon salt
poppy seeds

Place the flour, dry mustard and salt in a bowl. Rub in the margarine until the mixture resembles fine bread-crumbs. Stir in the grated cheese. Add sufficient water to give a soft not sticky dough. Knead the dough lightly and roll out on a lightly floured work surface. Stamp out 3 inch/7.5 cm biscuit shapes and place on lightly greased baking sheets. Beat egg, mix with salt and brush over biscuits. Sprinkle with poppy seeds and bake at 190°C/375°F/Gas 5 for 10 minutes.

The blue or green veins which occur in certain cheeses are due to the introduction of *penicillium glaucum* or *penicillium roqueforti* spores. These develop as the cheese ripens. This process sometimes happens naturally – as originally happened in the Roquefort caves – but usually the cheesemaker helps it along by piercing with fine stainless steel needles, for example. This aerates the paste and helps the veins in the cheese to spread.

Some blue cheeses have a naturally formed dry rind; others have almost no rind at all and then the surface is usually slightly sticky. These cheeses will not grate but they can be chopped or crumbled. There are also a number of soft blue cheeses which have a thin white rind rather like that of Camembert. For cooking, these cheeses need to have the rind removed and the curd cut into slivers. This is easier to do if the cheese is taken straight from the fridge.

I have made a fairly arbitrary division of the blue cheeses in the listing, into those which will just about crumble and those which definitely will not. The distinction is only really important for certain recipes.

Buying Guide

The firmer blue cheeses should be evenly veined. If they have a rind there should be no sign of brown discoloration beneath the rind, nor should the rind be too badly cracked.

Soft blue cheeses may be sold at various stages of their maturity. Young cheeses will be firmer and milder than fully mature cheeses.

Storing Guide

Wrap blue cheese in clingfilm or foil, making sure that all the air is excluded. This helps to keep the cheese in good condition and also keeps the smells away from other food in the fridge or pantry. If using the fridge, store in the vegetable compartment at the base.

Remember to remove from the fridge at least an hour before serving. Try not to keep taking the cheese in and out of the fridge as frequent changes in temperature cause quick deterioration.

Freezing blue cheese tends to detract from the flavour. However, it is possible to freeze small pieces of leftover cheese. Double wrap in foil and fast freeze. Thaw in the fridge and use up as quickly as possible.

Slicing and Serving

All blue cheese is easier to cut if you dip the cheese knife in very hot water and wipe dry before using.

CHEESES WHICH CRUMBLE

AMERICAN BLUE *(L)*: These cheeses were based on Roquefort but are made with pasteurised cow's milk. The best are Maytag, Nauvoo and Oregon Blue.

BEENLEIGH BLUE *(L)*: A semi-hard blue veined cheese made in Devon from unpasteurised milk of Friesland ewes.

BLEU D'AUVERGNE *(S)*: This French cheese is subject to an 'appellation controlée' which regulates its production. It has greenish-blue veins and a pinkish-brown rind which should be removed before eating. It has a full sharp flavour with a touch of saltiness.

BLUE CHESHIRE *(S)*: The veins of this lovely cheese are in fact distinctly green. This was a naturally occurring blue cheese called Green Fade but it wasn't reliable enough for commercial practicality. It is now helped along with stainless steel needles. The cheese has a soft crumbly texture and a very rich tangy flavour. Some afficionados declare that it is superior even to Stilton.

BLUE SHROPSHIRE *(S)*: This is a relatively new cheese which is made not in Shropshire but in Leicestershire. It has deep blue veins and a good yellow colour. It has a creamy texture and quite a strong flavour.

BLUE WENSLEYDALE *(L)*: This is close-textured cheese greatly sought after by some. It is only made in a very few dairies. It has a mild and delicate flavour.

DANISH BLUE *(E)*: A rindless crumbly cheese with very white curd and very blue veins. The flavour is quite strong. A milder version with a less sharp flavour is sold as Mellow Blue.

EDELPILZKÄSE *(S)*: Germany's best contribution to the blue cheese selection has a soft but slightly crumbly texture and a good sharp flavour.

FORME D'AMBERT *(S)*: Looks like a baby Stilton and has a similar rough grey crust. The paste is a smooth creamy white marbled with dark blue-green veining.

GORGONZOLA *(E)*: The veins of this Italian cheese are definitely green in colour. It has a natural brownish rind and a lightly piquant, full flavour.

MYCELLA *(S)*: This Danish cheese has a creamy soft curd with a whitish-brown crust. The cheese has a mature flavour which is milder and smoother than Danish Blue.

ROQUEFORT *(E)*: This king of French cheeses is made from ewe's milk and is subject to a cheese *'appellation controlée'*. It is one of the most expensive of the blue cheeses. It has greenish veining through an off-white curd. The cheese has no rind and can become rather crumbly at the edges. The flavour is lightly sharp but with a smooth roundness.

STILTON *(E)*: This is certainly the king of English cheeses. It can only be made in the three shires of Leicester, Nottingham and Derby. It is a medium-sized cylindrical cheese with a natural rough coat. The bluish-green veins are set in a pale ivory curd. The flavour is rich and creamy. A whole cheese should be cut in steps: it should not have the middle gouged out of it which results in dry cheese and wastage.

SOFT BLUE CHEESE

BAVARIA BLUE *(E)*: This German cheese is an invented cheese. It is made from milk with the addition of cream. The cheese is fairly small and has a white rind rather like Camembert. It has a pale creamy paste with patches of blue mould.

BLEU DE BRESSE or BRESSE BLEU *(S)*: This is a small round creamy cheese with a thin white rind. It has a very soft creamy texture but a slightly tangy flavour.

BLUE BRIE *(E)*: This was originally created in Germany but is now made in many European countries. It is thicker than Brie but has a similar white rind. There are patches of mould distributed through the creamy paste. It is fairly mild in flavour.

DOLCELATTE *(S)*: A toned-down version of Gorgonzola, this Italian cheese is deliciously mild and delicate. It has no rind and a smooth creamy texture with blue veins running through.

LYMESWOLD *(E)*: England's answer to Blue Brie, this soft cheese is even milder than its Continental counterparts. It has the same thin white rind and creamy texture.

LYS BLEU *(S)*: A long log with a white rind and delicate blue veins.

PIPO CRÈME *(S)*: A semi soft blue veined log rather similar to Lys Bleu.

MIXTURES

Mixtures of blue cheese and other plain or milder cheeses have become popular newcomers to the market place. Here are a few of the better known ones.

ADMIRAL'S: Cheddar with a layer of port and Stilton through the centre.

BLUE CRÈME: A mild creamy cheese layered with Danish Blue.

HUNTSMAN: Stilton layered with Double Gloucester.

ILCHESTER: Double Gloucester with a layer of Stilton through the centre.

TORTA: This is a traditional Italian cheese with layers of Gorgonzola and Mascarpone.

WALTON: Stilton mixed with Cheddar and chopped walnuts and coated with walnuts.

HOLIDAY CHEESES

When next in Austria look out for Tiroler Graukäse. It is made from pressed ripened sour-milk curds which are washed with *penicillium* moulds during the ripening period so that the moulds spread from the surface inwards, sometimes leaving the core unpenetrated.

Or in Spain seek out Cabarales, the country's major veined cheese. It may be made with cow's milk alone or cow's milk mixed with ewe's or goat's milk. It is a strong smelling cheese with a powerful flavour. It has a greyish red rind with a crust and a dull white curd with yellow-brown patches and irregular blue veining.

SNACKS, APPETIZERS AND CANAPÉS

Potted Blue Cheese

Stilton is the traditional cheese to be potted but most of the firmer, crumbly blue cheeses can be treated in this way. It's very rich but delicious with wholemeal rolls.

6 oz/175 g blue cheese
3 oz/75 g (⅓ cup) butter, softened
2 teaspoons port or brandy
pinch of ground mace or nutmeg

Cut the cheese into small pieces and mash in a bowl with 2 oz/50 g butter, the port or brandy and the spice. Press into small pots, and cover with the remaining butter after melting and clarifying.

Blue Cheese and Bacon Open Sandwich

Use any kind of blue cheese to hand.

8 rashers streaky (Canadian) bacon, rind removed
16 'no need to soak' prunes, stones removed
8 oz/225 g blue cheese
4 tablespoons (⅓ cup) mayonnaise
4 slices wholemeal bread
4 lettuce leaves
4 small tomatoes
4 spring onions (scallions), trimmed and finely sliced

Cut each rasher of bacon in half and roll around a prune. Grill under a moderate heat for 10 minutes, turning, then allow to cool. Crumble the blue cheese and mix 1 oz/25 g with the mayonnaise. Reserve the rest. Spread the mayonnaise mixture over the slices of bread and place a lettuce leaf on top. Slice tomatoes and place slices diagonally across the lettuce leaf. Place two bacon rolls together in opposite corners. Mix the sliced spring onion with the remaining cheese. Sprinkle mixture down tomatoes and serve.

Stilton Toasties

Here's a variation on Welsh Rarebit using blue cheese.

8 oz/225 g (2¾ cups) Stilton cheese, crumbled
1 teaspoon dry mustard powder
1 egg, beaten
pepper
1 tablespoon port (optional)
4 slices bread

Mix together the Stilton, dry mustard, egg and pepper to form a cheese paste. Add port, if using. Toast the bread on both sides, then spread the cheese paste evenly over one side of each piece of toast. Grill under a moderate grill for about 4 minutes or until the cheese has melted and is bubbly. Serve immediately.

Roquefort Tartlets

These tartlets make stunning finger food for parties.

Makes 12–14

1 × 7½ oz/215 g (½ lb) packet shortcrust pastry, defrosted

Filling
1 oz/25 g (¼ cup) walnuts, chopped
3 oz/75 g (1 cup) Roquefort cheese, crumbled
1 egg yolk
2 tablespoons (3 tbsp) double (heavy) cream

Roll out the pastry and use to line tartlet tins. Mix walnuts with cheese, egg yolk and double cream. Spoon into pastry cases and bake at 190°C/375°F/Gas 5 for 10–12 minutes. Serve warm.

Blue Cheese Filling for Tartlets or Vol-au-Vents

This is very good made with Danish Blue or with Stilton.

1 oz/25 g (⅛ cup) butter

1 oz/25 g (2 tbsp) plain (all-purpose) flour

¼ pint/150 ml (⅔ cup) milk

¼ pint/150 ml (⅔ cup) double (heavy) cream

4 oz/100 g (1⅓ cup) blue cheese, crumbled

freshly milled black pepper

12 plain or cheese pastry tartlets (see page 51) or 16–18 small cocktail vol-au-vents

Melt the butter in a saucepan and stir in the flour. Gradually add the milk and bring to the boil, stirring all the time. The mixture should be very thick. Stir in the cream and the cheese and season with pepper. When the cheese has melted into the mixture, leave it to cool. Spoon into tartlets or vol-au-vents as required.

Stuffed Dates and Prunes

This recipe makes delicious Christmas-time nibbles. Store in the fridge and bring out when guests arrive. Roquefort is the best to use.

2 oz/50 g (⅔ cup) blue cheese, crumbled

1 oz/25 g (1½ tbsp) butter, softened

2 teaspoons brandy

1 box dates or 8 oz/225 g (½ lb) 'no need to soak' prunes

Mash the cheese and butter together with a fork and then work in the brandy. Chill the mixture for 30 minutes. Slit open the dates or prunes and remove the stones. Press a little of the cheese mixture into the cavity of each one. Chill in the fridge before serving.

STARTERS AND SOUPS

Blue Cheese Terrine

Any kind of blue cheese can be used in this recipe but it was originally devised with Danish Blue in mind. Serve with crusty rolls or with wholemeal bread.

1 packet aspic powder
$\frac{1}{4}$ pint/150 ml ($\frac{2}{3}$ cup) boiling water
3 hard-boiled eggs, chopped
4 oz/100 g (1 cup) blue cheese, grated
$\frac{1}{4}$ pint/150 ml ($\frac{2}{3}$ cup) soured cream
1 egg, separated
2–3 celery stalks, blanched for 5 minutes in boiling water and very finely chopped

Place the aspic powder in a bowl and pour the boiling water over it. Stir until the crystals have dissolved then leave to cool, but do not allow to set. Mix the chopped hard-boiled eggs and cheese with the soured cream and egg yolk. Stir in the celery and the cooled aspic. Whisk the egg white until stiff and add a tablespoon to the cheese mixture. Then fold in the rest of the egg white. Spoon the mixture into a 1 lb/450 g loaf tin and place in the fridge to set. Turn out and serve cut into slices.

Stilton and Banana Truffles

The rather surprising combination of flavours in this recipe makes an unusual addition to any tray of canapés.

6 oz/175 g White Stilton
2 oz/50 g Blue Stilton
2 oz/50 g ($\frac{1}{3}$ cup) sultanas
1 banana, mashed
2 oz/50 g (1 cup) wholemeal breadcrumbs
1 dessert apple, peeled, cored and grated
1 teaspoon mild curry powder

Mix the cheeses with the sultanas and banana. Add the breadcrumbs, apple and curry powder to taste. Beat together with a wooden spoon to get a good blend. Roll portions of the mixture into small balls and serve with cocktail sticks.

Celery Sticks with Italian Torta

Using this deliciously creamy, layered Italian cheese saves mixing up your own combination of cheese. Alternatively mix any leftover blue cheese with cream cheese or quark and use in the same way.

1 head celery, trimmed and washed, with the toughest outer stalks removed
8 oz/225 g (½ lb) Italian Torta
paprika pepper

Cut the celery sticks into 2–3 inch/5–7.5 cm lengths. Mash the cheese with a fork and use to fill the lengths of celery. Sprinkle with paprika pepper to garnish.

Blue Cheese Cocktail Bites

Any kind of well flavoured blue cheese can be used in this recipe. Try Bleu d'Auvergne, Mycella or Blue Cheshire as well.

2 oz/50 g (¼ cup) butter
2 oz/50 g (⅓ cup) flour
½ pint/300 ml (1¼ cup) milk
3 oz/75 g (½ cup) Bel Paese cheese, cut into pieces
3 oz/75 g (¾ cup) blue cheese, grated or crumbled
salt and black pepper
2 eggs, beaten
dry breadcrumbs
oil for deep-frying

Heat the butter in a saucepan and stir in the flour and then the milk. Bring the mixture to the boil stirring all the time. When the mixture is really thick, stir in the cheeses and seasoning. Beat well together and transfer to a bowl. Leave to cool and then chill for at least an hour. Shape the mixture into small balls and double coat in egg and breadcrumbs. Deep-fry in batches in hot oil for 1–2 minutes until crisp and golden. Serve at once.

Blue Cheese Mousse

Serve this delicate mousse as a starter with fingers of toast. It's wonderful made with Dolcelatte, but you can use any soft creamy blue cheese.

1 teaspoon powdered gelatine

1 tablespoon water

6 oz/175 g (2 cups) soft creamy blue cheese

2 eggs, separated

$\frac{1}{4}$ teaspoon celery salt

pinch of cayenne pepper

1 tablespoon lemon juice

$\frac{1}{4}$ pint/150 ml ($\frac{2}{3}$ cup) double (heavy) cream

Sprinkle the gelatine over the water in a cup and allow to swell. Place the cheese, egg yolks, celery salt, cayenne pepper and lemon juice together in a bowl and beat until smooth. Add the double cream and whisk until thick. Dissolve the sponged gelatine over hot water and stir into the cheese mixture. Whisk egg whites until stiff and fold into the cheese mixture. Divide the mixture between four ramekin dishes and allow to set in the fridge.

Eggs in Moonshine

This makes an unusual starter at dinner, or it can be increased in quantity and served as a supper dish. In Victorian times the word 'green' used to be used to describe what we would call 'blue' cheese so any kind of blue cheese could be used in this recipe.

4 slices white bread

butter

4 eggs

salt and pepper

2 oz/50 g (1$\frac{1}{3}$ cup) Gorgonzola cheese, grated or crumbled

Cut rounds out of the centre of each slice of bread. Toast the rounds and butter them. Poach the eggs in an egg poacher and sprinkle each one with salt and pepper. When the eggs are cooked place on the buttered rounds of toast and scatter the cheese over the top. Serve hot just as the cheese begins to melt.

Celery Soup with Blue Cheese

Celery and blue cheese are an almost unbeatable combination. Any blue cheese can be used but you may need to use more if you are using up a mild Blue Brie or Lymeswold.

1 onion, sliced
$\frac{1}{2}$ oz/15 g (1 tbsp) butter
1 head celery, washed, trimmed and sliced
1 large potato, peeled and roughly chopped
1$\frac{1}{2}$ pints/900 ml (3$\frac{1}{2}$ cups) chicken or vegetable stock
1 oz/25 g (1$\frac{1}{2}$ tbsp) blue cheese, crumbled
freshly ground black pepper

Gently fry the onion in the butter until it turns transparent. Add the celery and continue frying gently for a further 3–4 minutes. Add the potato and stock and bring the mixture to the boil. Cover and simmer for 30 minutes. Purée in a blender or food processor along with the cheese, or rub through a sieve. Season with black pepper and return to the heat for 2–3 minutes before serving.

Soup Garnishes

Blue cheese garnishes can add interest to all kinds of soup.

Try crumbled gorgonzola on a slice of cucumber, thin slices of Lymeswold mixed with thinly sliced fennel, crumbled Roquefort with fried breadcrumbs, and crumbled Stilton mixed with chopped walnuts.

Stilton Soup

This is a deliciously rich soup. When entertaining, serve with hot herb bread or crusty brown rolls.

1 oz/25 g (1½ tbsp) butter
½ lb/225 g (2 cups) onions, peeled and chopped
½ lb/225 g (1⅓ cups) celery, washed, trimmed and chopped
¾ pint/450 ml (2 cups) water
1 chicken stock cube
½ teaspoon celery salt
ground black pepper
2 teaspoons cornflour (cornstarch)
½ pint/300 ml (1¼ cups) milk
½ lb/225 g (2⅔ cups) Stilton, rind removed, and grated or crumbled

Garnish
4 tablespoons single cream
2 slices white bread, fried in butter and diced

Melt the butter in a large heavy-based saucepan. Add the onion and celery and fry for 15 minutes over a gentle heat until soft. Add water, stock cube, celery salt and pepper. Bring to the boil, cover, and simmer gently for 15 minutes. Remove from the heat and blend in a liquidizer or food processor to make a purée, or rub through a sieve. Then return to the pan.

Blend the cornflour to a smooth paste with a little of the milk and add to the saucepan with the rest of the milk. Bring to the boil, stirring, and boil for 1 minute to thicken. Stir the Stilton cheese into the soup and heat to melt the cheese but do not allow to boil or the cheese may curdle. Serve hot with a swirl of cream and some croûtons scattered over.

MAIN COURSE DISHES

Pasta with Blue Cheese and Mushrooms

Here's a tasty way to keep the calories down with a low fat blue cheese. It makes a good supper dish.

6 oz/175 g (cup) button mushrooms, quartered

2 oz/50 g ($\frac{1}{4}$ cup) butter

$\frac{1}{2}$ oz/15 g (1 scant tbsp) flour

$\frac{1}{2}$ pint/300 ml (1 cup) low fat milk

5 oz/125 g ($1\frac{1}{2}$ cup) Blue Tendale cheese, grated

salt and pepper

12 oz/350 g fresh green egg noodles

2 tablespoons freshly chopped parsley

Toss the mushrooms in the melted butter for 2 minutes and remove with a draining spoon. Stir the flour into the fat and gradually add the milk to make a sauce. Bring to the boil and stir until thickened. Whisk in the cheese and season to taste. Add the mushrooms.

Cook the noodles in boiling salted water for 3–4 minutes and drain thoroughly. Stir into the cheese sauce and pour into a warm serving dish. Serve immediately, garnished with freshly chopped parsley.

Pasta Auvergne-Style

This recipe originally used Bleu d'Auvergne, but any kind of crumbly blue cheese can be used. I have used Blue Cheshire among others.

8 oz/225 g (½ lb) pasta (spaghetti, noodles or shapes)
1 teaspoon olive oil
4 oz/100 g (1 cup) blue cheese, crumbled
8 tablespoons (⅔ cup) soured cream
4 teaspoons (1½ tbsp) freshly chopped parsley
1 oz/25 g (¼ cup) walnuts, chopped
freshly milled black pepper

Cook the pasta in plenty of salted boiling water with a teaspoon of olive oil. It will take around 12–15 minutes, depending on the type of pasta used – check the packet for directions. When it is just tender drain well and return to the pan. Add all the remaining ingredients and toss over a high heat to warm through.

Blue Cheese and Broccoli Quiche

The vegetable filling for this quiche can be varied according to what is available. I have tried it with sliced and gently fried courgettes and with blanched fennel, and they were both very good.

1 × 7½ oz/215 g (½ lb) packet frozen shortcrust pastry, thawed
6 oz/175 g broccoli florets, blanched for 2 minutes in boiling water
3 eggs, beaten
¼ pint/150 ml (⅔ cup) double (heavy) cream
2–3 tablespoons (3–4 tbsp) milk
3 oz/75 g (¾ cup) firm plain cheese, grated
1 oz/25 g (⅓ cup) blue cheese, crumbled
freshly milled black pepper

Roll out the pastry and use to line an 8 inch/20 cm loose-based flan tin. Arrange the well drained broccoli florets in the base of the flan. Beat the eggs with the cream and milk, and stir in the cheeses and black pepper. Pour over the broccoli. Bake at 190°C/375°F/Gas 5 for 40–45 minutes until lightly browned and set in the centre.

Right: *Swiss Fondue (page 53).*

Crispy Haddock Lasagne

Here's a slightly different recipe for lasagne, using fish and blue cheese. I used Danish Blue, but any other blue cheese could be used. This recipe is quite substantial and will probably serve five to six people.

1 lb/450 g haddock

1 oz/25 g (1½ tbsp) butter

1 onion, peeled and chopped

1 tablespoon flour

½ pint/300 ml (1¼ cups) milk

1 × 7 oz/198 g can (2 cups) sweetcorn with red peppers, drained

4 oz/100 g (1 cup) blue cheese, crumbled

salt and freshly ground pepper

6 oz/175 g thin sheets no-cook lasagne

¼ pint/150 ml (⅔ cup) double (heavy) cream

¼ pint/150 ml (⅔ cup) unsweetened natural yogurt

1 large egg, beaten

1 teaspoon dried tarragon

1 small packet plain crisps, crushed

fresh parsley, to garnish

Poach the fish in just enough water to cover for 5–6 minutes. Measure ½ pint/300 ml of the cooking liquid and reserve (make up to ½ pint/300 ml with water if necessary). Remove skin and bones, and flake fish. Melt the butter in a large saucepan, gently fry onion until soft, then stir in the flour, milk and fish liquid. Bring to the boil, stirring continuously, until slightly thickened. Cook for 1 minute. Remove from the heat, add the fish, sweetcorn, cheese and seasoning.

Layer sauce and dry lasagne sheets in a large ovenproof dish (approx. 3 pints/1.75 litre capacity), finishing with a layer of sauce. Cover the dish with foil and bake at 190°C/375°F/Gas 5 for 25 minutes.

Mix the cream, yogurt, egg and tarragon together. Pour over the top of the lasagne to cover completely. Sprinkle with crisps. Bake uncovered for a further 15 minutes until the top is set and golden. Garnish with fresh parsley. Serve hot with salad and crusty bread.

Left: *Savoury Cheesecake (page 45).*

Chicken Breasts Dolcelatte

This is a delicious variation on the classic chicken Cordon Bleu.

4 large chicken breasts, skinned and boned
1 garlic clove
4 oz/100 g (1⅓ cup) Dolcelatte cheese
1 (size 3) egg, beaten
3 oz/75 g (1½ cups) breadcrumbs
oil for deep-frying

Make a cut horizontally through the centre of each chicken breast to form a deep pocket. Cut the garlic clove in half and rub the cut sides around the pocket in each chicken breast. Cut cheese into four equal pieces. Insert a piece of cheese into the pocket of each chicken breast. If you wish, secure this slit with a cocktail stick.

Dip each chicken breast into beaten egg and then coat with breadcrumbs. Chill until required. Deep-fry the chicken parcels in hot oil for about 12–15 minutes until the coating is golden brown and the chicken is cooked.

Steaks with Roquefort Cheese Sauce

This is an excellent dinner-party dish. Serve with jacket potatoes and a green vegetable or carrots.

This sauce also goes very well with grilled or fried chicken breasts.

1 oz/25 g (1½ tbsp) butter
4 × 8 oz/225 g steaks
2 tablespoons (3 tbsp) brandy
1 teaspoon cornflour (cornstarch)
6 tablespoons (½ cup) double (heavy) cream
4 oz/100 g (1 cup) Roquefort cheese, crumbled or grated
ground black pepper

Melt the butter in a frying pan, add the steaks and fry them according to taste, turning once during cooking.

Remove from the pan and keep warm. Add the brandy to the pan. Blend the cornflour with the cream and add to the pan, stirring. Add crumbled cheese and pepper to taste. Bring to the boil, stiring, and cook for 1 minute. Serve with the steaks.

Savoury Mille Feuilles

This unusual combination of blue cheese and chicken with layers of flaky pastry makes a lovely buffet dish. Use more or less blue cheese depending on the strength of flavour of the one you have available. Danish Blue is particularly good in this recipe.

1 lb/450 g puff pastry, thawed

milk

12 oz/350 g (2¼ cups) cold, cooked chicken meat, diced

½ green pepper, seeded and finely chopped

½ red pepper, seeded and finely chopped

2–3 oz/50–75 g blue cheese, at room temperature, skin removed if necessary

1 tablespoon mayonnaise

3 tablespoons (¼ cup) natural thick yogurt or soured cream

salt and ground black pepper

pinch of paprika

lemon juice to taste

cucumber twists, to garnish

Roll out pastry and cut into three 4½ × 10 inch/11 × 25 cm pieces. Prick thoroughly. Mark one piece into a criss-cross lattice pattern; this will form the top layer. Place pieces on a baking tray and chill. Brush marked strip only with milk, and bake the pieces at 220°C/425°F/Gas 7 for about 10 minutes until brown and cooked. Lift on to a wire rack and cool completely. Trim edges so that all three strips are the same size.

Mix the chicken cubes with the peppers. Beat the cheese until smooth and add all remaining ingredients. Gently stir in the chicken mixture. Place one piece of pastry on a serving dish and cover with half the chicken mixture. Place second piece of pastry on top and cover with remaining chicken. Top with final pastry piece. Garnish with cucumber twists.

ACCOMPANIMENTS AND SALADS

Potatoes with Blue Cheese

This idea comes from Italy where slices of Gorgonzola are often used.

1½ lb/675 g potatoes
butter
1 oz/25 g blue cheese (more if you are using a mild blue creamy cheese)
black pepper
1 tablespoon freshly chopped chives

Boil the potatoes in their skins until just tender. Peel, slice and arrange in a buttered entrée dish. Place in the oven at 150°C/300°F/Gas 2 and leave for 10 minutes. Cut the cheese into thin slices, or crumble, and arrange on top of the potatoes. Sprinkle with pepper and return to the oven for a further 10–15 minutes. Sprinkle with chives and serve.

Blue Cheese Slaw

This makes a delicious variation on the more unusual American coleslaw. Add a few walnuts for added interest. Use Stilton, Blue Cheshire or Blue Wensleydale.

¼ white cabbage, finely shredded
1 carrot, coarsely grated
4 oz/100 g (¼ lb) blue cheese
4 oz/100 g (½ cup) quark low-fat soft cheese
1 teaspoon cider or wine vinegar
milk
freshly ground black pepper

Mix the cabbage and carrot in a bowl. Mash the blue cheese with a fork and blend with the quark. Add the vinegar and sufficient milk to make a smooth creamy dressing. Season with pepper and pour over the salad. Toss and serve.

Blue Cheese and Mandarin Salad

This is an interesting salad to have on a buffet table, and it goes very well with a selection of cold meats such as roast beef, pork, chicken and ham. It also makes a good starter, in which case serve on a bed of shredded lettuce and with brown bread rolls.

Any kind of firm blue cheese can be used. If you can find mandarin orange segments in natural juice, they taste much nicer and do not contain so much sugar.

1 × 10 oz/298 g can mandarin oranges
3 oz/75 g (⅔ cup) blue cheese, crumbled
¼ pint/150 ml (⅔ cup) soured cream
salt and black pepper
1 lb/450 g white cabbage, shredded

Drain the juice from the mandarins into a bowl and add the cheese and soured cream. Beat very well together with a fork and season to taste. Mix the mandarins and shredded cabbage together in a large bowl and pour the blue cheese mixture over the top.

Blue Cheese Salad Dressing

Roquefort is the best blue cheese to use in salad dressings but Stilton, Gorgonzola and Danish Blue also work quite well. Go easy on the salt, though, or better still omit it altogether.

2 oz/50 g (½ cup) crumbly blue cheese
6 tablespoons (½ cup) olive oil
1 tablespoon sherry, white wine vinegar or lemon juice
freshly ground black pepper
milk

Place all the ingredients except the milk in a blender or food processor and blend until smooth. Add a little milk to thin the dressing if necessary.

Variation
A much lower-fat dressing can be made by substituting 4 tablespoons of quark low-fat soft cheese for 5 tablespoons of the olive oil. More milk may be necessary in this version. Keep tasting the dressing as you mix it.

BAKING

Blue Cheese Rolls

Rolls made with cheese are fairly unusual but made with blue cheese they are even rarer. This recipe was originated with Lymeswold but any kind of soft blue cheese such as Blue Brie, Bavaria Blue or Dolcelatte could be used.

Makes 8

$\frac{1}{4}$ pint/150 ml ($\frac{2}{3}$ cup) light ale or lager
$\frac{1}{2}$ level tablespoon dried yeast
1 tablespoon soft brown sugar
$\frac{1}{2}$ oz/15 g (1 tbsp) white vegetable fat or lard
12 oz/350 g (2 cups) wholewheat flour, sifted
$\frac{1}{2}$ teaspoon salt
3 oz/75 g ($\frac{2}{3}$ cup) soft blue cheese, diced
2 teaspoons milk

Warm the beer until it is at blood temperature. Sprinkle on the yeast and stir in half the sugar. Leave to stand in a warm place for 10–15 minutes until frothy.

Rub the fat into the flour and stir in the remaining sugar and the salt. Make a well in the centre and pour in the yeast mixture. Mix to a soft dough and knead for 5 minutes. Leave to stand in a warm place for about 30–40 minutes until doubled in size.

Knock back the risen dough and knead in the blue cheese. Divide the dough into eight portions and roll each one into a ball. Place in a round or square cake tin so that the rolls just touch but are not squashed together.

Leave to rise in a warm place until doubled in size. Brush the rolls with milk and bake at 200°C/400°F/Gas 6 for 20 minutes or until they are firm to the touch and sound hollow when tapped underneath. Leave to cool on a wire rack and break apart to serve.

These cheeses are correctly known as soft paste cheeses. They are a mature or ripened form of simple soft cheeses. The paste usually softens as it matures and the flavour intensifies. If the cheese is kept correctly it will mature from the outside towards the centre. They may form a washed or a flowery rind. These cheeses are usually small in depth and diameter – with the exception of Brie and one or two others.

When cooking with soft matured cheeses, you may need to remove a thick rind – in this case increase the quantity of cheese by an ounce or so.

Buying Guide

Test by pressing your finger gently on the wrapped cheese. It should be springy to the touch. The centre of the cheese may still be firm and indeed it is probably better to buy young cheese and let it mature at home to the degree you require. Some cheeses which are 'running away' on the cheese counter have been kept at too high a temperature. Avoid any cheeses with a slimy or mouldy rind.

Storing Guide

If the cheese is very young and you want it to mature a little keep at room temperature. Store matured soft cheeses in the box in which it is packed or double-wrap in foil or clingfilm and then in a polythene bag. Keep near the base of the fridge. Cheese stored in its original box will keep for 1–2 weeks but once it has been cut it should be used within 2 or 3 days. Remember to take the cheese out of the fridge half an hour before you want to eat it.

To prevent mature soft cheeses from running after they have been cut, place them cut side-up in their boxes or press a strip of wood against the cut surface.

For freezing, cut into the sizes that you are likely to use at one go. Thaw at room temperature and use as soon as possible after thawing.

Slicing and Serving

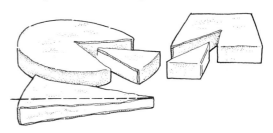

BELLE DES CHAMPS *(S):* This delicately mild French cheese with an aerated paste will just about slice and should perhaps more correctly be listed under semi-hard cheeses. However, it melts in the mouth and behaves on cooking far more like a soft matured cheese than a semi-hard cheese.

BEL PAESE *(E):* The name of this lovely round and creamy Italian cheese was inspired by Father Antonio Stoppani's book *Il Bel Paese* (*Beautiful Country*). The paste is very pale in colour and has a buttery taste and the cheese has a shiny golden rind. Though perhaps not strictly speaking a soft paste cheese, it behaves like one on cooking. Tiny round processed variations of the cheese wrapped in silver paper are also on sale in most supermarkets.

BRIE *(E):* This is a classic soft paste cheese from France. It is large and flat with a creamy texture and soft white rind. It is usually sold in wedges. It has a mild flavour which strengthens on maturing. At the shop the creamy centre has a tendency to start running out of the cheese. There are a variety of different kinds of Brie. French ones include Brie de Meaux and Brie de Melun. German versions of Brie tend to be smaller and thicker and some are flavoured with mushrooms or green peppercorns.

CAMEMBERT *(E)*: These small 4 inch/10 cm French cheeses are rich and creamy and have a soft white rind similar to Brie. The cheese itself is thicker and stronger in both aroma and flavour. Some cheeses are sold in halves or sixths. Like Brie, the cheese gets quite runny and much more pungent when mature.

CAPRICES DES DIEUX *(E)*: This factory-made double cream cheese has a white rind and a mild flavour. It is sold in small oval boxes.

CHAMOIS D'OR *(S)*: Shaped like Brie, this French cheese is similar but creamier. It has a white mould rind and a creamy paste.

CHAUMES *(S)*: See Semi-Hard Cheeses.

COULOMIERS *(S)*: This French cheese is very similar to Brie, but is smaller in size.

LIMBOURG *(S)*: This small square or rectangular cheese has a distinctive pungent flavour and a deep yellow colour. It was originally made in Belgium but it now generally considered to be a German cheese.

LIVAROT *(S)*: This small round French cheese has a bright orange washed rind and a strong pungent flavour. It is sold wrapped in reeds.

MELBURY *(E)*: This is a relatively new English cheese which ripens from a mild-tasting cheese with a slightly crumbly centre to a mellow flavour with a soft creamy texture. It is encased in a thin white mould crust and looks a little similar to Chamois d'Or.

MUNSTER *(S)*: This small square French cheese has a deep yellow rind with a yellow paste. It has a pungent aroma and flavour when ripe. It is one of the French cheeses which carries an *'apellation d'origine'* to show that it is the genuine article.

PONT L'EVEQUE *(S)*: This famous cheese from the village in Normandy has a smooth yellow-washed rind and is usually square in shape. The paste is yellow and soft with quite a strong taste which strengthens even more with maturity.

REBLOCHON *(S)*: This is another French speciality cheese from the Haute-Savoie. However it is also made over the border in Italy. The cheese is sold between two paper-thin wooden discs. It has a firm pinkish-brown rind and a creamy buttery paste. It has a mild fruity flavour which matures to a slightly bitter taste.

SAINT ALBRAY *(E)*: This relatively new French cheese could also be placed in the sliceable cheese section but, in cooking, it behaves more like a soft paste cheese. It is a full fat cheese with a washed mould rind. Both rind and curd are yellow in colour and the cheese is shaped like a scalloped ring. It has a fairly mild flavour.

SAINT NECTAIRE *(S)*: This French cheese is made in the Auvergne. It has a pale orange rind and a creamy colour. The flavour is mild and nutty.

TALEGGIO *(S)*: This Italian cheese has been made since the eleventh century on the plain of Lombardy. It has a smooth texture and a mild, though full, flavour. It has a thin rind which may be pink or grey in colour.

PROCESSED CHEESES

There is a very wide range of processed cheeses on sale, some from the UK, others from France, Germany and Scandinavia. Many of them are flavoured with herbs, spices, fruit, nuts or shellfish. They all mix well into sauces and cooked dishes, and behave very much like soft matured cheeses. Processed cheese is cooked and so does not continue to mature.

Of particular interest are the French walnut and grapeseed cheeses. The walnut version is very creamy and is encrusted with walnut halves. There is sometimes also a centre layer of nuts. The grapeseed cheeses are a speciality of Savoy, and have a rind made from roasted grapeseeds pressed together. The cheese itself, which is processed Emmental, has a very mild flavour and the grape seeds are nutty and crunchy in texture.

Storing Guide

Processed cheese keeps for quite a long time in a cool place or in the fridge. Once the packaging has been opened it should be wrapped in foil and eaten within a week or so.

SNACKS, APPETIZERS AND CANAPÉS

Cheesy Choice Open Sandwich

This recipe makes eight small Danish open sandwiches. Any kind of soft mature or semi-hard cheese can be used with the Danish Blue.

4 oz/100 g (1½ cups) Melbury or Brie, thinly sliced
4 large slices rye bread, buttered and cut in half
8 small lettuce leaves
4 oz/100 g (1⅓ cups) Danish Blue cheese, chopped
1 tablespoon flaked almonds
8 small pickled gherkins, cut into fan shapes

Use the sliced cheese to cover each slice of bread. Place a lettuce leaf on top of each one and weight down in place with a little blue cheese. Sprinkle with flaked almonds and garnish with gherkin fans.

Brie and Mushroom Potato Filling

Brie and the other soft cheeses melt very easily into a sauce. Here it's used to make a delicious topping for jacket baked potatoes.

2 rashers streaky (Canadian) bacon
½ oz/15 g (1 tbsp) butter
2 oz/50 g (⅔ cup) mushrooms, sliced
3 tablespoons (¼ cup) mayonnaise
1 tablespoon cornflour (cornstarch)
¼ pint/150 ml (⅔ cup) milk
6 oz/175 g (1 cup) Brie, sliced thinly
1 teaspoon mixed herbs
celery salt
pepper
4 jacket potatoes, baked in the oven

Grill the bacon under a moderate grill until crisp. Cut into ¼ inch/6 mm pieces. Melt the butter and fry the mushrooms for 2–3 minutes until soft. Add the mayonnaise. Blend the cornflour with the milk and add to the pan. Stir the sauce to thicken and then stir in the cheese, mixed herbs, celery salt and pepper to taste.

Cut a cross in the top of the jacket potatoes, spoon over the sauce and sprinkle with chopped bacon.

Fried Apples with Cheese

This recipe makes an excellent brunch or breakfast snack. It was originally devised for Belle des Champs but you could use Chaumes or Saint Albray.

4 green eating apples, cored and sliced
4 oz/100 g (⅔ cup) soft matured cheese, thinly sliced
4 slices hot toast

Place the slices of apple in a non-stick frying pan without oil and brown over a medium heat. As the apples become soft, cover with the slices of cheese. As soon as the cheese begins to melt pick up sections of the apple and cheese mixture with a fish slice and transfer to pieces of hot toast. Serve at once.

Camembert and Sesame Spread

Spread on pieces of fried bread, cut into shapes and mix with the Melbury and Olive Canapés.

1 oz/25 g (⅛ cup) sesame seeds
8 oz/225 g (1⅓ cups) Camembert
2 oz/50 g (¼ cup) butter, softened
1 tablespoon brandy
2 tablespoons (3 tbsp) soured cream

Toast the sesame seeds under the grill, stirring to brown them evenly. Remove from the grill and leave to cool. Mash all the remaining ingredients together and beat until well mixed. Stir in the sesame seeds and beat again.

Melbury and Olive Canapé Spread

*For a stronger flavour use one of
the other matured soft cheeses.*

3 tablespoons ($\frac{1}{4}$ cup) pimento-stuffed olives
8 oz/225 g (1$\frac{1}{3}$ cups) Melbury cheese, with or without crust
soured cream to moisten
black pepper

Cut the olives and cheese into small pieces and place
all the ingredients in a food processor. Process until
smooth. If you do not have a food processor or if you
prefer a slightly more crunchy effect, chop the olives
as finely as possible. Mash the cheese with a fork and
mix in the olives. Add soured cream to smooth the mixture and to give the desired consistency. Season. Use
to spread on any kind of canapé base.

Camembert Puffs

*Use Brie, Melbury or any other soft
cheese.*

Makes 20

1 × 7$\frac{1}{2}$ oz/215 g ($\frac{1}{2}$ lb) packet puff pastry, thawed
1 egg, beaten
poppy seeds

Camembert filling
1 oz/25 g (1$\frac{1}{28}$ tbsp) butter
1 oz/25 g (2 tbsp) flour
$\frac{1}{4}$ pint/150 ml ($\frac{2}{3}$ cup) milk
3 × 1$\frac{1}{2}$ oz/40 g Camembert triangles or 5 oz/150 g ($\frac{3}{4}$ cup)
   Camembert, finely sliced

Roll out the pastry on a lightly floured surface and cut
into 2 inch/5 cm wide strips. Cut each strip on the dia-
gonal to make about twenty diamond shapes. Place on
a dampened baking sheet, brush with beaten egg and
sprinkle with poppy seeds. Bake at 220°C/425°F/Gas
7 for 6–8 minutes until golden. Remove from oven.
   To make the filling, melt the butter in a pan. Add
the flour and cook for 1 minute. Gradually stir in the
milk and bring to the boil, stirring. Add the sliced cheese

and continue cooking over a gentle heat to slowly melt the cheese. Carefully cut the diamond shapes in half horizontally and place a teaspoonful of the Camembert mixture into each puff. Place lid on top.

To reheat puffs, place them in the oven set at 300°F/150°C Gas 2 for 5 minutes.

STARTERS AND SOUPS

Melbury Salad

Brie, Camembert or any other soft matured cheeses can be used in this recipe. They are best used when they are fairly unripe.

1 smoked trout
6 oz/175 g (1 cup) Melbury cheese
2 tomatoes, sliced
1 courgette (zucchini), thinly sliced
2–3 lettuce leaves, finely shredded

Dressing:
juice and grated rind of 1 lemon
1 teaspoon olive oil
$\frac{1}{4}$ teaspoon dried thyme
freshly ground black pepper

Skin the trout and carefully remove the flesh, making sure that there are no bones attached. Arrange on one side of four small serving plates. Remove the crust and cut the cheese into thin slices. Arrange a row of cheese slices opposite the trout. Next place a few slices of tomato and courgette at each end and place rows of finely shredded lettuce along the centre line between the trout and the cheese. Mix all the dressing ingredients together and pour over the salads. Serve at once.

Saint Albray Salad

The rind is traditionally included in this tasty French salad.

1 head Italian fennel, very finely sliced
4 oz/100 g (¼ lb) French beans, topped and tailed
1 small head spring greens or green cabbage
6 oz/175 g (1 cup) Saint Albray cheese, cubed

Dressing
3 tablespoons (¼ cup) olive oil
2 teaspoons (3 tsp) wine vinegar
½ teaspoon tomato ketchup
1 tablespoon freshly chopped parsley
2 spring onions (scallions), very finely chopped
pinch of dry mustard
pinch of curry powder

Blanch the vegetables in boiling water for 3 minutes, then refresh in cold water. Drain well and toss in a bowl with the cheese.

Mix all the dressing ingredients and beat well with a fork. Pour over the salad and serve.

Deep-Fried Camembert with Gooseberry Sauce

It is essential that these Camembert wedges are cooked in very hot oil for a very short time. If the temperature is too low the cheese will melt and the breadcrumbs will become soggy.

1 whole Camembert, weighing about 8 oz/225 g (½ lb)
1 egg, beaten
2 oz/50 g (1 cup) white breadcrumbs
oil for deep-frying

Sauce
12 oz/350 g (¾ lb) gooseberries, toppped and tailed
1 tablespoon water
1 oz/25 g (1½ tbsp) sugar

Cut the Camembert cheese into eight equal wedges. Coat first with beaten egg and then with breadcrumbs.

Place on a plate and chill in a cold fridge or freezer for 30 minutes.

To make the sauce, place the gooseberries in a pan with the water and sugar. Bring to the boil and simmer gently for 20 minutes until fairly thick. Sieve to remove skins.

Heat oil in a deep-fat fryer or large saucepan until very hot. Fry four wedges in the hot oil for 30–40 seconds until light golden brown. Drain on absorbent paper and repeat with the remaining Camembert pieces. Serve with gooseberry sauce.

Artichoke Bases with Cheese

This recipe can also be made with artichoke hearts, but this makes a slightly more substantial dish. Use Brie or Melbury.

1 × can 12 artichoke bases, drained and quartered
2 egg yolks
½ pint/300 ml (1¼ cups) single (light) cream
4 oz/100 g (⅔ cup) soft matured cheese
black pepper

Place the artichoke bases in a shallow heatproof dish or divide them between four ramekin dishes. Beat the egg yolks and mix into the cream. Remove the crust from the cheese, cut into slivers and arrange on top of the artichokes. Pour on the egg and cream mixture. Sprinkle with pepper and bake at 150°C/300°F/Gas 2 for 25–30 minutes until lightly set. Serve at once.

Belgian Cheese Fondue

The stronger the cheese used, the better Belgian Fondue is. If you are making this delicious dish for a number of people, its a good idea to make two batches using different cheeses – strong Camembert or Munster and a mixture of Bel Paese and blue cheese. Serve with a good home-made tomato sauce or tomato relish.

4 oz/100 g ($\frac{1}{2}$ cup) cornflour (cornstarch)

8 fl. oz/225 ml (1 cup) milk

1$\frac{1}{2}$ lb/675 g ripe Camembert

4 oz/100 g ($\frac{1}{2}$ cup) butter

salt and pepper

nutmeg

flour

2 large (size 1) eggs, beaten

2–3 oz/50–75 g ($\frac{2}{3}$ cup) dry breadcrumbs

oil for deep-frying

Mix the cornflour with a little of the milk to form a smooth paste, then gradually stir in the rest. Pour into a saucepan. Remove all the rind from the cheese, cut into pieces and add to the pan with the butter, salt, pepper and nutmeg. Cook slowly, stirring all the time until the mixture is really thick and comes away from the sides of the pan. The mixture may go through a phase when it looks just like scrambled eggs, but keep stirring. When the mixture is really thick spread out on a tray so that the paste is about 1$\frac{1}{2}$–2 inches/4–5 cm thick. Leave to cool and solidify.

Cut the paste into the shapes required (cubes or triangles, say), and dust with flour. Next dip in beaten egg and then in breadcrumbs, making sure that the breadcrumbs completely cover the cheese mixture. You can double coat with both egg and breadcrumbs to be absolutely sure of the fondue not splitting during cooking, but this will require more coating ingredients. Deep-fry in batches in hot oil for 1–2 minutes until crisp and golden. The centre should be runny when cut.

Soft Cheese and Onion Soup

The more mature the cheese you use in the soup the stronger flavoured it will be!

1½ oz/40 g (2 tbsp) butter
1 large onion, very finely chopped
1 oz/25 g (2 tbsp) flour
½ pint/300 ml (1¼ cups) chicken stock
¾ pint/450 ml (2 cups) milk
4 oz/100 g (⅔ cup) soft cheese, rind removed
black pepper
fried bread croûtons

Melt the butter in a saucepan and very gently fry the onion to soften it. Do not allow to brown. Stir in the flour and gradually add the stock and the milk, stirring all the time. Bring the mixture to the boil and simmer for 15 minutes. Cut the cheese into small pieces and add to the soup. Stir until they have dissolved. Season with pepper and serve with fried bread croûtons.

Sweetcorn and Cheese Soup

Use any kind of mild matured soft cheese in this very quick-to-make soup: Brie, Melbury or Camembert would be good.

2 × 7 oz/190 g cans creamed sweetcorn
¾ pint/450 ml (2 cups) milk
4 oz/100 g (⅔ cup) matured soft cheese, crust removed
salt and pepper
pinch of nutmeg
freshly chopped parsley

Spoon the sweetcorn into a pan and gradually stir in the milk. Cut the cheese into small pieces and add to the soup with the salt, pepper and nutmeg. Stir over a medium heat until all the cheese has melted and the soup has thoroughly heated through. Serve with a sprinkling of freshly chopped parsley.

Bean and Camembert Soup

This is another quick-to-make soup. It will take a more mature cheese than some of the others.

1 onion, finely chopped
$\frac{1}{2}$ green pepper, seeded and finely chopped
1 tablespoon cooking oil
1 sherry glass dry or medium sherry
1 × 14 oz/400 g can red kidney beans
1 pint/600 ml ($2\frac{1}{2}$ cups) chicken stock
1 teaspoon paprika pepper
$\frac{1}{2}$ teaspoon dried thyme
salt and pepper
3 oz/75 g ($\frac{1}{2}$ cup) well matured Camembert, rind removed

Quickly fry the onion and green pepper in hot cooking oil to soften and brown slightly. Pour on the sherry and bring to the boil. Add the contents of the can of beans, the stock, paprika, thyme and seasoning and bring to the boil. Simmer for 20 minutes. Cut the cheese into pieces and add to the soup. Stir until melted. Correct the seasoning and thin with a little milk if necessary.

Mushroom Soup

Mushrooms make a lovely soup but they do need a little extra substance and this is provided by the cheese.

1 lb/450 g mushrooms, chopped
1 small onion, chopped
1 oz/25 g ($1\frac{1}{2}$ tbsp) butter
$1\frac{1}{4}$ pints/750 ml ($3\frac{1}{4}$ cups) chicken stock
3 oz/75 g ($\frac{1}{3}$ cup) matured soft cheese, crust removed
pinch of dried thyme
garlic salt
black pepper
freshly chopped parsley

Gently fry the mushrooms and onion in the butter to soften. Add the stock, bring to the boil, and simmer for 15 minutes. Purée in a blender or liquidize with the cheese, cut into small pieces. Return to the pan and add the thyme, garlic salt and black pepper to taste. Reheat and serve, sprinkled with chopped parsley.

MAIN COURSE DISHES

Lasagne with Bel Paese

On cooking, Bel Paese melts to give a creamy sauce-like effect. This can be used to cut out one of the stages in the making of a vegetarian lasagne.

8 sheets no-cook lasagne

5 oz/150 g ($\frac{1}{3}$ cup) Bel Paese, cut into slices

Vegetable sauce

1 onion, finely chopped

1 tablespoon cooking oil

1 green pepper, seeded and diced

2 courgettes (zucchini), finely diced

1 × 14 oz/400 g can tomatoes, coarsely chopped

1 tablespoon tomato purée

salt and pepper

Start by making the vegetable sauce. Gently fry the onion in the oil. When it becomes transparent, add the pepper and continue to cook gently for 4–5 minutes to soften the vegetables. Add the courgettes and cook for a further minute or so. Stir in the contents of the can of tomatoes, the tomato purée and seasonings. Layer the sauce with the sheets of lasagne and the slices of Bel Paese in a heatproof entrée dish, starting with the pasta and ending with sauce and cheese. Bake at 200°C/400°F/Gas 6 for 35–40 minutes.

Crêpes au Fromage

Use the basic pancake recipe given on page 150 for Crespolini and make up into twelve or sixteen small crêpes. Some French recipes use a large (size 1) egg or add a teaspoon of olive oil to the crêpe mixture. Use Brie or Camembert, for preference.

12–16 crêpes, kept warm
2 oz/50 g ($\frac{1}{2}$ cup) Parmesan cheese, grated

Filling
1$\frac{1}{2}$ oz/40 g (2 tbsp) butter
1 oz/25 g (2 tbsp) flour
$\frac{1}{2}$ pint/300 ml (1$\frac{1}{4}$ cups) warm milk
1 small onion, peeled
1 carrot, peeled
1 bay leaf
salt and pepper
6 oz/175 g (1 cup) soft matured cheese, rind removed

To make the filling, melt the butter in a pan and stir in the flour. Pour on the milk and bring to the boil, whisking all the time with a wire whisk. When the mixture boils add the onion, carrot, bay leaf and seasonings, and reduce the heat. Simmer for 5 minutes. Remove the vegetables and the bay leaf and stir in the cheese, cut into small pieces. Use this mixture to fill the pancakes. Roll up and place in a buttered heatproof dish and sprinkle with the grated Parmesan. Melt the cheese under a hot grill.

Variation
This filling is also very good piped into croissants which have had the horns cut off and holes bored through the croissants.

Baked Casserole of Sole Fillets

This rather unusual recipe comes from Italy and is usually made with Bel Paese cheese. However any kind of mild soft cheese can be used.

3 oz/75 g ($\frac{1}{3}$ cup) butter
2 oz/50 g ($\frac{1}{3}$ cup) flour
1 pint/600 ml (2$\frac{1}{2}$ cups) milk
4 oz/100 g ($\frac{2}{3}$ cup) mild soft cheese, cut into cubes
black pepper
2 eggs
12 fillets lemon or Dover sole, skinned (3 fish)
2 tablespoons (3 tbsp) freshly chopped parsley
salt
1 oz/25 g ($\frac{1}{4}$ cup) Parmesan cheese, grated

Melt the butter in a pan and stir in the flour. Gradually add the milk, stirring all the time. Bring to the boil, and simmer for 1–2 minutes. Stir in the soft cheese and continue stirring until it is well mixed in. Add the black pepper and then whisk in the eggs with a wire whisk. Spoon this sauce into the base of a well buttered heat-proof entrée dish. Sprinkle the fillets of sole with the chopped parsley and salt. Roll up and arrange round the outside of the casserole on top of the sauce. Push down slightly. Sprinkle with Parmesan and bake at 190°C/375°F/Gas 5 for about 40 minutes. Serve with grilled or baked tomatoes.

Cheesy Seafood Scallops

Use any combination of shellfish and firm white fish in this interesting variation on a popular theme. Use the milder cheeses such as Brie or Melbury with delicately flavoured fish and a stronger cheese such as Camembert with smoked fish, celery or mussels.

8 oz/225 g ($\frac{1}{2}$ lb) filleted white fish (haddock, plaice or monk-fish)

3–4 tablespoons ($\frac{1}{4}$ cup) milk

8 oz/225 g (1$\frac{1}{3}$ cups) mild soft cheese

$\frac{1}{4}$ pint/150 ml ($\frac{2}{3}$ cup) single (light) cream

black pepper

6 oz/175 g (1 cup) peeled prawns (shrimps)

1 oz/25 g ($\frac{1}{2}$ cup) fresh breadcrumbs

1 oz/25 g ($\frac{1}{4}$ cup) Parmesan cheese, grated

Poach the fish in the milk for 6–8 minutes until tender. Strain off the liquid into another pan. Flake the fish and remove any skin or bones. Cut the crust off and cut the cheese into slices. Add to the pan with the milk and also add the cream and black pepper. Heat gently, stirring all the time until the cheese melts. Bring to the boil and simmer to thicken a little. Add the fish and shellfish and toss in the sauce. Spoon into scallop shells or small flat heatproof dishes. Sprinkle the centre with a mixture of breadcrumbs and Parmesan cheese. Place under a hot grill for 2–3 minutes until lightly browned.

Plaice Parfait

Use one of the milder matured soft cheeses such as Melbury or Brie for this recipe. Sole can be used instead of plaice.

4 large or 8 small fillets plaice

6 tablespoons ($\frac{1}{2}$ cup) milk

2 tablespoons (3 tbsp) dry vermouth

salt and pepper

4 oz/100 g ($\frac{2}{3}$ cup) mild soft cheese

1 teaspoon cornflour (cornstarch)

4 tablespoons ($\frac{1}{3}$ cup) double (heavy) cream

2 oz/50 g ($\frac{2}{3}$ cup) button mushrooms, sliced

2 oz/50 g ($\frac{1}{3}$ cup) prawns (shrimps)

freshly chopped parsley, to garnish

Roll up the plaice fillets with the skin on the inside of the roll. Place the rolls in a shallow ovenproof dish and pour on the milk and vermouth and seasonings. Cover with foil and bake at 180°C/350°F/Gas 4 for 20–25 minutes until just cooked. Remove from the oven and strain off the cooking juices into a saucepan. Keep the fish warm.

Cut the cheese into pieces and remove the crust. Add to the pan with the fish juices. Stir over a low heat until the cheese melts. Mix the cornflour with the cream and add to the pan with the mushrooms. Bring the mixture to the boil, stirring all the time. Cook for 2–3 minutes. Stir in the prawns and pour over the fish. Garnish with freshly chopped parsley.

Chicken Breasts with Brie

Any kind of matured soft cheese can be used in this recipe.

4 chicken breast fillets
salt and pepper
1 lb/450 g fresh or frozen asparagus

Sauce
$\frac{1}{4}$ pint/150 ml ($\frac{2}{3}$ cup) double (heavy) cream
4 oz/100 g ($\frac{2}{3}$ cup) Brie, crust removed
2 tablespoons (3 tbsp) brandy
1 tablespoon chicken stock or white wine

Season the chicken fillets with salt and pepper and roll up. Wrap first in clingfilm and then in foil, twisting the ends of the wrappings to give a good thick sausage. Place in a pan of gently boiling water and simmer for 30 minutes. Steam the asparagus in a deep saucepan with a very little water in the base. Cook until tender. Drain and keep warm.

Pour the cream into a saucepan and place over a gentle heat. Add all the remaining sauce ingredients, having cut the cheese into small pieces. Bring slowly to the boil, stirring all the time, then season to taste.

Unwrap the chicken and cut into rounds. Arrange on a plate with the asparagus and pour the sauce over the top. Serve at once.

ACCOMPANIMENTS AND SALADS

Brie, Mushroom and Potato Savoury

Any soft cheese works well in this recipe, although I used Brie. It's up to you whether you remove the rind or not.

1½ lb/675 g potatoes, peeled and sliced
6 oz/175 g (2 cups) button mushrooms, sliced
6 oz/175 g (1 cup) soft cheese, thinly sliced
salt and pepper
3–4 tomatoes, peeled and sliced
butter

Layer the potatoes, mushrooms and cheese in a pie dish, seasoning as you go. End with a layer of potatoes. Arrange the tomatoes over the top and dot with butter. Bake at 190°C/375°F/Gas 5 for about an hour until the potatoes are tender. Serve with salad.

Creamy Potato Hotpot

Smoked bacon improves the flavour of this dish but green bacon can be used if preferred. Use any soft cheese, but Brie is good.

6 rashers smoked streaky (Canadian) bacon, rinded and diced
1 large onion, finely chopped
4 oz/100 g (1⅓ cups) soft cheese, rind removed
2 lb/900 g potatoes, peeled and sliced
black pepper
8 fl oz/225 ml (1 cup) milk
a little grated nutmeg

Fry the bacon in its own fat for 2–3 minutes. Add the onion and continue frying for a further 3–4 minutes until lightly browned. Slice the cheese and layer in a shallow entrée dish with the sliced potatoes. Start and finish with the potatoes, and sprinkle each layer of potato with the bacon and onion mixture and a little black pepper. Pour on the milk and sprinkle with nutmeg. Bake at 190°C/375°F/Gas 5 for about an hour.

Cheese made from goat's milk is growing in popularity, and as a result more people are producing it. Indeed hardly any time seems to go by without another small producer offering a new goat's cheese. Goat's cheese has a very distinctive flavour and this flavour seems to characterise almost all cheeses made with goat's milk, though some are much stronger than others. The flavour is a mixture of sharpness and mustiness, and its intensity usually depends upon the youth or maturity of the cheese.

There is quite a variety of goat's cheese on the market, and they can have almost any texture from smooth and waxy to hard and crumbly. Some of them may have a waxy coating, others form a mould on the rind, and some have no rind or coating of any kind.

The youngest and freshest goat's cheese available is probably chevret frais. This is rather like fromage frais or quark made from cow's milk. It is quite mild in flavour. The choice also includes a variety of soft cheeses which are produced without any rind, though they may have a coating of herbs or ash. The latter tends to dry the cheese, making it sweeter and easier to digest.

Next come the soft cheeses which are encased in a rind of some kind. Some of these form a mould after a few days. However, this does not impair the flavour and is perfectly harmless. These soft goat's cheeses come in all shapes and sizes from simple rounds and logs to complex geometric shapes.

There are also a number of hard goat's cheeses. These too vary in shape and size from very small hard drum shapes to large rindless cheeses which are stored in brine.

Goat's milk is exceptionally high in fat content. It is also free from many of the pathogens that affect cow's milk. This is one of the reasons why it is hardly ever pasteurized.

The ratio of rind to cheese in goat's cheese is quite high and you may lose as much as 1 oz/25 g in every 4 oz/100 g. The quantities given in the recipes for goat's cheese *include* the rind.

Buying Guide

Most of the more generally available goat's cheeses come from France. However specialist cheese shops and some supermarkets do stock home-produced goat's cheese as well as those from other countries. Many of them can also be bought where they are made, so look out for local advertisements. Fresh and soft goat's cheeses should be clean-looking and free from mould. They are usually fairly soft to the touch and should not smell too highly. Pure goat's milk cheese is usually only made from the beginning of spring to the end of autumn. Those available during the winter will have been stored or been made from a mixture of goat's and cow's milk.

Storing Guide

Fresh goat's cheese will keep for 2 or 3 days in a cool place. Soft cheeses will keep for up to a week or more in a cool larder. Remember to bring up to room temperature before serving.

Hard goat's cheeses will usually keep for longer. However, Halloumi cheese should be stored in brine. It will keep for 5–6 days after the pack is opened, provided that it remains in its brine.

Slicing and Serving

Most goat's cheeses are fairly easy to cut and serve. However, cutting into one of the pyramid shapes can be a problem for guests. Overleaf is a drawing to show how to cut it for them on request.

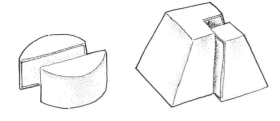

FIRM CHEESES

ALLERDALE *(L)*: Made at Wigton in Cumbria, this semi-hard cheese has a mellow flavour. It is made in flattish rounds weighing about 2 lb/900 g. Not available all the year round.

CHEVROTIN DES ARAVIS *(S)*: Sometimes sold as Tomme de Chèvre, this is a small round disc with a smooth surface and firm consistency. Sometimes made from a mixture of goat's and cow's milk. It has a fairly prominent flavour.

RIBBLESDALE *(L)*: A smooth though slightly crumbly cheese from Lancashire which has a very mild goat flavour. It keeps for 2 or 3 weeks, maturing slightly.

SALTERLEIGH *(L)*: A firm pressed cheese made in Devon. It has a rich full flavour.

WHARFEDALE BLUE *(L)*: This is said to be Britain's first blue goat's cheese.

SOFT CHEESES

BANON *(S)*: A small round French cheese wrapped in chestnut leaves. It is also made from cow's and ewe's milk and comes from Provence.

BÛCHE DE CHÈVRE *(E)*: Often just known as goat or chèvre log, this is a soft French cheese which is made in a long log shape. It has a rind which grows a downy white mould as it matures. To cook with this cheese, peel off the rind in one piece and scrape off any bits of cheese that remain in the rind.

CHABICHOU *(E)*: A small log cheese sometimes known simply as Chabi.

CHÈVRE BLANC *(E)*: Another large log or long triangle which may be covered in ash or dill or have a downy rind. Similar soft fresh goat's cheese is flavoured with garlic and sold as a Garlic Log.

PYRAMID CHÈVRE *(E)*: There are various types of pyramid or truncated pyramid-shaped goat's cheese including Pontigny Saint Pierre, Cendre and Valençay. The former is made in the Berry province of France and its production is controlled by law. It is dry cured for a month. Cendre and Valençay on the other hand are covered in ash. Others have a white or yellow rind.

SAINT CHRISTOPHE *(S)*: A small log cheese from Berry in France. It has straw running through the middle to stop it breaking up.

SAINTE-MAURE *(S)*: Another small log from Touraine. This cheese is matured in damp caves, thus gaining a downy white or green mould.

THREE SHIRES *(L)*: Made in Northamptonshire, this small cheese may be coated in poppy seeds, herbs or ash.

VULSCOMBE *(L)*: Another small English goat's cheese made in Devon. It may be flavoured with herbs, pepper or garlic.

HOLIDAY CHEESES

Others to look out for when you are on holiday include Bruscion, a small cylindrical cheese from Switzerland with a particularly piquant flavour; and Cadiz Malaga and Camerano from Spain. The latter is moulded in a small basket.

In Italy the choice includes Broccio, a very fresh unsalted cheese and Brucialepre, a soft cheese with a thin rind and white bloom. An interesting cheese from France is Charolais – not as one might expect from the milk of Charolais cattle but from goats grazing on the Charolais hills of Burgundy.

Further north Sweden and Norway offer Getmesost and Gjetost. These are not really cheeses as they are made from goat's milk whey. They have a strong condensed flavour and are usually fairly hard. In the other direction Masnor is a Balkan cheese also made from goat's milk whey. It is shaped like an elongated pear with a thin smooth skin and a dense texture.

STARTERS AND SOUPS

Chèvre Kiwi Salad

Use a small log of goat's cheese for this recipe. The younger the cheese the better. Leave the rind in place. If you can only get hold of the larger logs, slice thinly and cut each slice in turn into half-moon shapes.

1 or 2 thick carrots, sliced in 16 uniform slices
salt
4 tablespoons ($\frac{1}{3}$ cup) olive oil
8 oz/225 g ($\frac{1}{2}$ lb) Chèvre log
4 kiwi fruit, peeled and sliced
1 teaspoon lemon juice
1 tablespoon orange juice
a little grated orange rind
salt and pepper
sprigs of Continental parsley

Cook the carrots in lightly salted water for 15–20 minutes until tender. Drain and toss in a little of the oil. Keep on one side. Slice the Chèvre log fairly thinly to make sixteen slices. Arrange alternate slices of Chèvre, kiwi fruit and carrot in a crescent around three-quarters of each serving plate. Mix the remaining oil with the lemon and orange juices. Stir in a little grated orange rind and seasoning. Pour over the salad. Decorate with sprigs of Continental parsley.

Goat's Cheese and Bacon Salad

Just increase the quantities to turn this attractive starter into a main meal salad.

4 rashers streaky (Canadian) bacon
a few curly endive leaves
1 small head radicchio
1 small head chicory
4 oz/100 g ($\frac{1}{4}$ lb) soft goat's cheese, sliced
4 walnut halves, chopped

Dressing

4 tablespoons ($\frac{1}{3}$ cup) walnut or olive oil

1 tablespoon wine or cider vinegar

a little grated orange rind

salt and pepper

Grill the bacon until crisp and chop coarsely. Arrange the various salad leaves on four small plates. Place slices of goat cheese on each and then sprinkle with walnuts and bacon. Mix all the dressing ingredients together and pour over the top.

Stuffed Figs

This is not a dessert but a very attractive starter. The figs should be as ripe as possible.

12 ripe figs

4 oz/100 g ($\frac{1}{2}$ cup) fresh goat's cheese (Chevret Frais), or 3 oz/75 g ($\frac{1}{3}$ cup) creamy goat's cheese beaten into 1 oz/25 g yogurt

salt and freshly ground black pepper

Dressing

4 tablespoons ($\frac{1}{3}$ cup) olive oil

1 dessertspoon white wine vinegar

pinch of dried crushed rosemary

salt and pepper

Wash and dry the figs. Cut off any stalks and cut into the figs with a deep cross across the top. Open up the figs as much as possible, without splitting them at the base. Mix the cheese with salt and pepper and spoon a little into the centre of each fig. Arrange three stuffed figs on each serving plate. Mix all the dressing ingredients and pour over the figs. Serve at once.

Tomato Chèvre

Almost any kind of goat's cheese can be used in this recipe.

6 tomatoes, cut in half in a zig-zag pattern
shredded lettuce leaves
1 bunch watercress
4 oz/100 g ($\frac{1}{4}$ lb) goat's cheese, chopped or grated
4 spring onions (scallions), finely chopped
10–12 grapes, seeded and finely chopped
1 tablespoon plain yogurt
salt and pepper

Spoon out the seeds and centres of the tomato halves and arrange three on a bed of shredded lettuce on four plates. Decorate with a few sprigs of watercress. Chop the remaining watercress and mix with the cheese, spring onions, grapes and yogurt, and season to taste. Spoon the mixture into the centre of each tomato half. Serve with a little more yogurt on the side.

Grilled Mushroom Caps

This simple dish makes a very good dinner-party starter. Serve with a good tomato-based relish.

24 medium mushroom caps
1 oz/25 g ($1\frac{1}{2}$ tbsp) butter
1 tablespoon freshly chopped chives

Filling
1 small onion, very finely chopped
1 garlic clove, crushed
1 tablespoon cooking oil
mushroom stalks, chopped
$\frac{1}{4}$ green pepper, very finely chopped
5 oz/150 g ripe goat's cheese, rind removed
2 tablespoons (3 tbsp) freshly chopped parsley
freshly ground black pepper

Arrange the mushroom caps on a baking tray. Dot with some of the butter and lightly grill for 8–10 minutes to soften them. Meanwhile fry the onion and garlic in cooking oil with the mushroom stalks until the onion turns transparent. Add the pepper and continue frying until all the vegetables are lightly browned. Remove from the heat and stir in the goat's cheese, cut into small pieces. Mix well together and add the parsley and black pepper. Place spoonfuls of the filling mixture on each mushroom cap. Dot with a little more butter and return to the grill. Cook for 3–4 minutes. Sprinkle with freshly chopped chives just before serving.

Kohlrabi and Cheese Soup

I used a large creamy goat's cheese log in this recipe but any kind of soft or fresh cheese could be used.

1 small onion, sliced
1 tablespoon cooking oil
3 tablespoons ($\frac{1}{4}$ cup) medium sherry
1 lb/450 g kohlrabi, peeled and sliced
1 medium potato, chopped
$1\frac{1}{2}$ pints/900 ml ($3\frac{1}{2}$ cups) chicken stock
3–4 oz/75–100 g ($\frac{2}{3}$ cup) goat's cheese
salt and pepper
freshly chopped parsley

Gently fry the onion in cooking oil until it turns transparent. Add the sherry and bring to the boil. Add the kohlrabi, potato and stock and return to the boil. Simmer for 30 minutes. Remove the rind and stir the cheese into the soup. Purée the soup in a blender or rub through a sieve. Add seasoning to taste and reheat. Serve with a little chopped parsley sprinkled on top.

MAIN COURSE DISHES

Stir-Fried Cheese with Mixed Vegetables

Take care not to cook the cheese for too long. It does not run but it can go quite tough. This dish can also be made with Halloumi cheese.

2 tablespoons (3 tbsp) cooking oil
4 spring onions (scallions)
$\frac{1}{2}$ inch/1.25 cm fresh root ginger, peeled and grated
4 oz/100 g (1 cup) carrots, cut into thin sticks
$\frac{1}{4}$ small Chinese cabbage, shredded
2 courgettes (zucchini), thinly sliced
1 oz/25 g ($\frac{1}{2}$ cup) Chinese beansprouts
4 oz/100 g (1 cup) hard goat's cheese, cut into thin strips
freshly ground black pepper

Heat the oil in a deep frying pan or wok and stir-fry the onions, ginger and carrots for 1–2 minutes. Add the Chinese cabbage, courgettes and beansprouts and continue stir-frying for 3–4 minutes until the vegetables are just beginning to soften. Add the cheese and black pepper and toss over a medium heat for 1 minute. Serve at once with rice or noodles.

Right: *Pasta with Blue Cheese and Mushrooms (page 95).*

Stuffed Swiss Chard

If you cannot find Swiss chard use large spinach leaves in pairs.

8 Swiss chard leaves
5–6 (½ cup) tablespoons tomato juice

Filling
2 oz/50 g (¼ cup) long-grain brown or white rice
4 fl. oz/100 ml (½ cup) water
salt
2 oz/50 g (⅓ cup) pine kernels
1 large onion, finely chopped
1 tablespoon cooking oil
1 small red pepper, seeded and finely chopped
4 oz/100 g (1⅓ cups) firm goat's cheese, chopped
2 tablespoons (3 tbsp) freshly chopped parsley
1 teaspoon freshly chopped mint
pinch of ground coriander
salt and pepper

Cut the stalks off the chard leaves and keep them on one side. Blanch the leaves in boiling water for a minute. Refresh in cold water.

Cook the rice in the boiling salted water for 12 minutes until all the water has been absorbed. The rice does not need to be fully cooked. Toast the pine kernels under the grill or in a dry frying pan. Fry the onion in the cooking oil. Add the red pepper and continue frying gently for 3–4 minutes. Finely chop the reserved chard stalks and add to the pan. Cook for a further minute or so, then add the cooked rice, toasted pine kernels, cheese, herbs, spice and seasoning. Place spoonfuls of the mixture in the centre of each Swiss chard leaf. Fold up like a parcel and if necessary secure with a cocktail stick. Place in a shallow heatproof baking dish and pour on the tomato juice. Cover with foil and bake at 180°C/350°F/Gas 4 for 35–40 minutes.

Left: *Savoury Mille Feuille (page 99).*

Noisettes of Veal or Pork with Goat's Cheese Sauce

This makes a very quick and easy dinner-party dish. Make the sauce in advance and finish off between courses.

4 shallots, very finely chopped
1 oz/25 g (1½ tbsp) butter
¼ pint/150 ml (⅔ cup) dry white wine
4 tablespoons (⅓ cup) double (heavy) cream
3 oz/75 g (⅓ cup) soft goat's cheese
black pepper
1 tablespoon olive oil
1 lb/450 g fillet of veal or pork, cut into thick rounds

Gently fry the shallots in half the butter for 2–3 minutes to soften. Do not allow them to brown. Add the white wine and bring to the boil. Simmer for 10–15 minutes to reduce the liquid by about half. Stir in the cream. Cut the rind off the goat's cheese and cut into small pieces, and gradually add to the sauce, with the pepper. Return to the boil and cook until the sauce reaches the desired consistency.

Meanwhile, heat the oil with the remaining butter in a frying pan and fry the noisettes of veal or pork for about 5–6 minutes on each side, depending on which meat you're using. Pour the sauce over the top of the meat in the pan, stir in all the cooking juices, and serve immediately.

Goat's Cheese, Herb and Potato Flan

This is one of my favourite potato dishes. It makes a good meal in itself if served with mixed salad and bread rolls. Use a large soft log cheese.

1 × 7½ oz/215 g (½ lb) packet frozen shortcrust pastry, thawed
8 oz/225 g (½ lb) potatoes, boiled and sliced
2 tablespoons (3 tbsp) freshly chopped parsley
1 tablespoon freshly chopped tarragon
7 oz/200 g (½ lb) goat's cheese, rind removed
3 eggs, separated
2 tablespoons (3 tbsp) double (heavy) cream
black pepper

Preheat the oven to 200°C/400°F/Gas 6. Roll out the pastry and use to line an 8 inch/20 cm loose-based flan tin. Prick the base very well all over and bake blind (with beans, greaseproof or foil) for 15 minutes. Line the half-cooked flan with sliced potatoes and sprinkle with herbs. Beat the goat's cheese together with the egg yolks, cream and pepper. Whisk the egg whites and stir a spoonful or two into the cheese mixture. Fold in the rest. Pour the mixture over the potatoes and stand on a baking tray. Reduce the oven temperature to 180°C/350°F/Gas 4, and bake for 40–45 minutes until golden on top.

Goat's Cheese with Spaghetti

This recipe makes a delicious variation on Spaghetti Carbonara. Do not add any salt to the recipe.

8 oz/225 g ($\frac{1}{2}$ lb) spaghetti (or other pasta)

1 teaspoon olive oil

1 oz/25 g (1$\frac{1}{2}$ tbsp) butter

6 oz/175 g (1 cup) streaky (Canadian) bacon, chopped

6 oz/175 g goat's cheese

6 eggs, beaten

4 tablespoons ($\frac{1}{3}$ cup) milk

freshly ground black pepper

Cook the spaghetti with the olive oil in plenty of boiling water until *al dente*. Melt the butter in another large pan and fry the bacon until lightly browned. Remove rind from the goat's cheese and beat with all the remaining ingredients to a smooth cream. Drain the spaghetti very well and add to the pan with the bacon. Pour on the egg and cheese mixture and toss the spaghetti over a gentle heat until the eggs thicken. Serve with a green salad.

ACCOMPANIMENTS AND SALADS

Broccoli with Goat's Cheese Sauce

The delicate flavour of this sauce also complements lightly poached white fish.

1 lb/450 g broccoli, trimmed
salt
1 oz/25 g (1½ tbsp) butter
1 oz/25 g (2 tbsp) flour
¾ pint/450 ml (2 cups) milk
3 oz/75 g goat's cheese log
black pepper

Cook the broccoli in a very little lightly salted boiling water for about 10–15 minutes until just tender. Transfer to a heatproof dish. Meanwhile melt the butter in a pan and stir in the flour. Gradually add the milk and bring to the boil, stirring all the time. Remove the rind from the goat's cheese and crumble into the sauce and stir until all the cheese has dissolved. Return to the boil, add the pepper and pour over the broccoli.

Winter Salad with Hard Goat's Cheese

Use one of the hard French or English goat's cheeses or Halloumi for this.

4 or 5 leaves of green cabbage or spring greens, stalks removed
1 large carrot, grated
2 oz/50 g (1 cup) Chinese beansprouts
2–3 oz/50–75 g (⅓ cup) hard goat's cheese, finely chopped

Dressing
2 tablespoons (3 tbsp) olive oil
1 teaspoon orange juice
1 teaspoon cider vinegar
salt and black pepper
a little grated orange rind

Very finely slice the cabbage leaves or spring greens. Mix with the grated carrot and beansprouts. Toss and pile into a salad bowl. Top with the chopped goat's cheese. Mix all the dressing ingredients together and pour over the salad. Chill for 20 minutes and serve.

Hungarian Salted Salad with Goat's Cheese

Use one of the hard French or English goat's cheeses or Halloumi in this recipe.

$\frac{1}{4}$ white cabbage, finely shredded
salt
4 inch/10 cm piece cucumber, very finely sliced
1 green pepper, seeded and shredded
$\frac{1}{4}$ teaspoon caraway seeds
3 oz/75 g ($\frac{1}{3}$ cup) hard goat's cheese, shredded
6–8 radishes

Dressing
1 tablespoon cooking oil
1 tablespoon wine vinegar
1 tablespoon milk
black pepper

Place the shredded cabbage in a bowl and sprinkle liberally with salt. Leave to stand for 1 hour. Treat the sliced cucumber and green pepper in the same way but in separate bowls. Wash each of the vegetables very well and drain on kitchen paper. Mix the cabbage with the caraway seeds and goat's cheese and place in mounds on a large serving plate. Add mounds of cucumber and green peppers. Add radishes, either sliced or cut into flowers. Mix all the dressing ingredients together and pour over the top.

These cheeses represent the simplest form of cheese and they are made in great variety in creameries and on farms and smallholdings. These unripened cheeses are characterized by a slightly acidic flavour and a soft spreadable texture. On cooking they tend to mix well into the surrounding ingredients. They have a high moisture content and a variable fat content, and these two factors form the basis for their classification into cream cheese, double cream cheese, full-fat soft cheese, medium-fat soft cheese, low-fat soft cheese and skimmed milk soft cheese.

Buying Guide

Soft cheeses must above all be fresh. Do not buy from shops which are unlikely to have a high turnover. If you are buying from large tubs at a delicatessen counter check to see that the cheese is not drying out, and it's also worth asking to smell a little of it – defects tend to show up in the smell.

Storing Guide

Soft cheeses are made to be consumed as soon as possible after purchase. Those packed in tubs or in foil will have a sell-by date, and the cheese should be eaten within a day or two of that date.

Store this kind of cheese in its own packaging near the top of the fridge. Do not keep for too long. It freezes very well. Wrap the packaged cheese in foil or in a heavy duty polythene bag and fast freeze. Thaw in the fridge and eat as soon as possible.

BAKER'S (L): This American fresh cheese is widely used in the bakery trade – hence its name. It is smooth and soft with a slightly sour taste. It is usually made from skimmed milk and is therefore low in fat.

BELLSHIRE (S): This is a new soft-textured cheese from one of the English dairies. Difficult to categorize, for it will just about slice, it has a similar flavour to fresh soft cheese, and cooks in much the same way. It is flavoured with chives and onions and is made from a base similar to White Stilton.

BOURSIN (E): This is a triple cream cheese which may be plain but is more usually flavoured with garlic and herbs or pepper.

CABOC (S): This small Scottish double cream cheese is rolled in pinhead oatmeal. It has a very mild and creamy flavour.

CAMBRIDGE (L): This is a traditional English soft cheese. It is rectangular in shape and sits in a straw base. It has an extra creamy layer running through the centre. It is made from whole milk and is unsalted.

COLWICK (L): This is similar to Cambridge but it is made in a flat round mould and the finished cheese has turned up edges. The curd may be lightly sprinkled with salt.

COTTAGE CHEESE (E): Cottage cheese as we know it today is an American-style cottage cheese and quite different from the traditional British cottage cheese (see page 00). There is no official definition of cottage cheese in the UK but it can be described as a low-fat soft cheese with a mild flavour and crumbly or slightly chunky texture. Cottage cheese is made from skimmed milk and may be flavoured with herbs or fruit.

CREAM CHEESE (E): This cheese must contain no less than 45 per cent milk fat. Double cream cheese contains no less than 65 per cent. The cheese has a soft buttery flavour with a rich, full and mildly acid flavour. It is usually made from cream and milk.

CROWDIE *(S)*: One of the oldest of Scottish cheeses. It is very soft and comes in cartons like quark. Sometimes flavoured with mild garlic or may be mixed two parts Crowdie to one part fresh double cream.

DEMI-SEL *(E)*: Square fresh cream cheese originally from Normandy in France. It has a mild, slightly salted flavour.

FRENCH HERB CHEESES *(E)*: These are made from fresh cream cheese. They are blended with herbs and garlic. Some have the herbs running through the cheese. Others are rolled to give a Swiss roll or roulade effect, sometimes known as Roulé.

FULL-FAT SOFT CHEESE *(E)*: The regulations state that these cheeses should contain not less than 20 per cent milk fat, and Philadelphia cheese is probably the best example. It is made from single cream and milk.

HOME-MADE CHEESES: See pages 168–174. These cheeses can be used in any of the recipes in this section.

LIPTAUER *(L)*: This is the German name for a cheese produced in Hungary. It is a soft dense ewe's milk cheese.

LOW-FAT SOFT CHEESE *(E)*: This type of cheese must contain less than 10 per cent but not less than 2 per cent milk fat. Many of the supermarket cheeses labelled curd cheese usually fall into this category. (There are also categories for medium-fat soft cheese – less than 25 per cent but not less than 10 per cent milk fat – and skimmed milk soft cheese, less than 2 per cent milk fat.)

MASCARPONE *(L)*: This is a very rich Italian cream cheese which looks rather like clotted cream.

NEUFCHÂTEL *(S)*: This soft and delicate French cheese is made with skimmed or whole milk and may sometimes be enriched with cream. It has a lovely fresh flavour and is often used in French cooking.

PETIT SUISSE *(E)*: This is unsalted and shaped like a small cylinder. It is often used for desserts.

QUARK (or QUARG) *(E)*: This is a type of soft cheese produced in Germany and some other parts of the Continent. Quark can vary in its fat content, but most of it is fat-free. It is a smooth white product with a mild, acid flavour. It is usually sold in tubs. The French version is known as fromage frais.

RICOTTA *(L)*: This is not a cheese in the strict sense of the word, for it is made from the milk whey rather than the curds. However, it is often enriched with milk or cream. Ewe's milk whey was the original base but cow's milk whey is also used. The texture is slightly crumbly and the cheese is snow-white in colour. It is used extensively in Italian cooking.

SAINT MORET *(S)*: This is a cream cheese from South Western France. It has a creamy texture and comes in a tub.

SNACKS, APPETIZERS AND CANAPÉS

Curried Cottage Cheese with Watercress

Pitta bread makes a very good base for open sandwiches. Split into two or for a much more substantial snack, use the whole thing.

4 Middle Eastern or pitta breads
2 oz/50 g (¼ cup) butter
bunch of watercress
4 sliced pineapple rings
8 oz/225 g (1 cup) cottage cheese
1 teaspoon curry powder
4 tablespoons (⅓ cup) raisins
1 avocado, stoned, peeled and sliced
paprika

Spread the bread with butter and arrange the watercress on the bread. Place the pineapple rings in the centre. Mix the cottage cheese with the curry powder and raisins and spoon over the pineapple. Decorate with slices of avocado and sprinkle with paprika.

Liptauer Korozott

Liptauer is a fresh curd cheese made from goat's or ewe's milk. It owes its name to the Liptau range of hills in Czechoslovakia where it is made. It is always served as Liptauer Korozott or garnished cheese. Use home-made or fairly acid soft cheese. Serve with cheese biscuits or thin slices of wholemeal bread

8 oz/225 g (1 cup) full-fat soft cheese
4 oz/100 g (½ cup) butter, softened
4 capers, finely chopped
1 teaspoon paprika pepper
½ teaspoon dry mustard
½ teaspoon freshly chopped chives or spring onion (scallion)
¼ teaspoon caraway seeds
1 tablespoon beer

Rub the cheese through a sieve. Cream the butter, mix in the cheese and beat until smooth. Add the remaining ingredients and beat again. Pile into a mound on a serving dish and serve with cheese biscuits or bread.

Jacket Potatoes with Fresh Cheeses

Fresh soft cheeses make an excellent base for making all kinds of flavoured toppings for jacket potatoes.

Try mixing cheese with freshly chopped herbs, diced crispy bacon, sweetcorn kernels, smoked flaked fish, chopped spring onion (scallion) or diced ham and peas. A really quick topping is simply to melt slices of ready flavoured cheese such as Bellshire or Boursin directly on to the potato.

Crab Rangoon

This is a South-East Asian speciality which makes an excellent cocktail snack. Buy the spring-roll or won-ton wrappers at any Chinese grocer. Alternatively, use very thinly rolled out shortcrust pastry. The effect will not be quite the same but the flavour is still good.

6 oz/175 g ($\frac{3}{4}$ cup) white crab meat
6 oz/175 g ($\frac{3}{4}$ cup) cream or curd cheese
1 teaspoon fruity sauce
$\frac{1}{2}$ garlic clove, crushed
salt and pepper
30–40 spring-roll wrappers
fat for deep-frying

Mix the crab meat, cheese, sauce and garlic to a paste and season to taste. Place small amounts in the centre of each wrapper. Pick up the four corners, and pinch the paste together to form a little sack, and carefully open out the top in a frill. The wrappers must be very well pinched together or the filling will come out during fry up. Place in the deep-fryer tray and lower into hot fat for about 2–3 minutes until crisp and brown.

Cottage Cheese and Parma Ham Canapés

Use this delicious mixture to fill small cocktail tartlets or to spread on Ritz crackers or fried bread croûtons. Add a little quark or cream cheese to help bind the mixture for the flat canapés.

8 oz/225 g (1 cup) cottage cheese
4 oz/100 g (¼ lb) Parma ham, fat removed, finely chopped
1 tablespoon freshly chopped mint
salt and freshly ground black pepper

Mix all the ingredients together in a bowl and season to taste.

VARIATIONS

Use 1 tablespoon freshly chopped parsley or chopped walnuts instead of mint.

Cheese Truffles

Cheese-based truffles make an unusual addition to a tray of mixed canapés. Here is a basic recipe using a variety of types of cheese with fresh cheeses. Choose one or more of the items from the list of flavourings to add to the base, and a complementary coating.

Makes approx. 32

BASIC RECIPE

4 oz/100 g (1 cup) hard, semi-hard or soft cheese, grated or
    mashed (Gouda, Tilsit, Brie)
4 oz/100 g (1⅓ cups) savoury biscuit crumbs
4 oz/100 g (½ cup) cream cheese or quark
salt and pepper

FLAVOURINGS	COATINGS
Raisins with grated orange rind	Chopped walnuts
Chopped dates	Toasted almond flakes
Chopped nuts	Chopped parsley
Chopped watercress and mustard	Paprika pepper
Cranberry sauce or chutney	Sesame seeds
Horseradish	Poppy seeds

Place all the ingredients together in basin. Add the flavouring of your choice and mix well together. Season to taste. Shape into small balls and roll in your chosen coating. Keep chilled until required.

Cream Cheese Fritters

This recipe originally used Ricotta cheese but any kind of really smooth cream or curd cheese can be used. Add a tablespoonful of finely grated hard cheese to the mixture for a more cheesy flavour.

8 oz/225 g (1 cup) cream cheese
3 oz/75 g ($\frac{1}{2}$ cup) flour
1 teaspoon baking powder
1 large egg
salt and black pepper
1 tablespoon brandy
1 teaspoon grated lemon rind
fat for deep-frying

Mash the cream cheese with a fork and then mix in all the other ingredients very thoroughly. Chill and then drop teaspoonfuls into hot fat and cook for 2–3 minutes until golden. Sprinkle with salt to serve.

CHEESE DIPS

Cream cheese, quark and fromage frais all make excellent bases for dips. Simply mix them with yogurt or milk to dilute, and flavour with garlic, chopped chives and spring onions, or with curry spices.

Spicy Cheese Dip

Serve with mixed vegetable crudities.

4 oz/100 g ($\frac{1}{2}$ cup) cream cheese or quark
1 tablespoon tomato purée
$\frac{1}{4}$ pint/150 ml ($\frac{2}{3}$ cup) mayonnaise
1 tablespoon mango chutney
1 small onion, grated
$\frac{1}{2}$ teaspoon mild curry powder or garam masala

Beat the cheese with the tomato purée and mayonnaise. Cut up any large pieces of mango in the chutney and add to the mixture with the onion and curry powder. Mix well together and spoon into a serving bowl.

Avocado and Cheese Dip

Serve with small cheese biscuits.

4 oz / 100 g ($\frac{1}{2}$ cup) cream cheese or quark
4 tablespoons ($\frac{1}{3}$ cup) soured cream
1 large avocado, peeled and stoned
juice of $\frac{1}{2}$ lemon
salt and pepper
2 tablespoons (3 tbsp) chopped walnuts

Mash the cheese with a fork and mix with the soured cream. Mash the avocado and add to the mixture with the lemon juice, and season to taste. If the mixture is not very smooth, rub through a sieve or process in a blender or food processor. Serve sprinkled with nuts

Chilli Bean Dip

Serve with Mexican Tortilla Chips.

1 × 8 oz / 225 g can butter beans, very well drained
6 oz / 225 g ($\frac{3}{4}$ cup) cream cheese or quark
1 small onion, grated
$\frac{1}{4}$ green pepper, seeded and finely chopped
$\frac{1}{2}$–1 teaspoon chilli powder or 6–7 drops Tabasco sauce
yogurt (optional)

Mash the beans with a fork and mix with the cheese. If the mixture is not very smooth, rub through a sieve or process in a blender or food processor. Stir in the onion, pepper and chilli powder or Tabasco to taste. If the mixture is too thick, thin with yogurt.

Michoteta

This is a traditional appetizer from Egypt. It can be made with Feta cheese as well.

4 oz / 100 g ($\frac{1}{2}$ cup) cottage cheese
juice of $\frac{1}{2}$ lemon
1 tablespoon olive oil
$\frac{1}{4}$ large cucumber, finely diced
1 very small onion, finely chopped
pinch of ground cumin
salt and black pepper

Place the cheese in a bowl with a tablespoon of water, and crumble with a fork. Slowly add the lemon juice and the oil, beating with a fork all the time. Stir all the remaining ingredients and season to taste.

STARTERS AND SOUPS

Neufchâtel Frappé

This is a sophisticated starter which should really impress your friends, if they are anything like mine!

8 oz/225 g (1 cup) Neufchâtel cheese
$\frac{1}{4}$ pint/150 ml ($\frac{2}{3}$ cup) natural yogurt
$\frac{1}{4}$ pint/150 ml ($\frac{2}{3}$ cup) double (heavy) cream
1 teaspoon orange juice
salt and freshly ground black pepper
2 oz/50 g ($\frac{1}{2}$ cup) broken walnuts

To serve
a few lettuce leaves
1 tomato, cut into thin wedges
French toasts or Melba toast

Blend the Neufchâtel, yogurt, double cream and orange juice together with a fork or in a blender. Season to taste. Add walnuts and mix thoroughly. Place in a container approx. 7 inches/18 cm square. Cover and freeze.

Remove from the freezer about 1$\frac{1}{2}$ hours before serving, and leave at room temperature. Scoop out and serve on finely shredded lettuce with thin tomato wedges, accompanied by French toasts or Melba toast.

Prawn Pots

This is an unusual variant of the straightforward potted shrimps. It comes from a friend who used to live in Morecombe Bay and bought fresh shellfish regularly.

12 oz/350 g (¾ lb) peeled prawns (shrimps), minced
4 oz/100 g (½ cup) cream cheese
4 oz/100 g (½ cup) unsalted butter, melted
4 spring onions (scallions), very finely chopped
¼ teaspoon nutmeg
salt and pepper

Mix the minced prawns and cream cheese with half the melted butter until thoroughly blended. Add the spring onions, nutmeg and seasoning and mix again. Spoon into four individual pots or ramekin dishes and top with the remaining melted butter. Place in the fridge to set. Serve with fingers of brown toast.

Celery and Cheese Mousse

This is one of my favourite dinner-party starters.

8 oz/225 g (½ lb) celery, trimmed and sliced
½ pint/300 ml (1 cup) chicken stock
5 oz/150 g (⅔ cup) full-fat soft cheese or quark low-fat soft cheese
½ oz/15 g (2 tbsp) gelatine
1½ tablespoons (2 tbsp) water
1 egg, separated
celery salt
black pepper
½ lemon, very finely sliced

Boil the celery in the chicken stock for about 30 minutes until very tender. Sieve or purée in a blender with all the cooking liquor. Gradually add the cheese and beat to a smooth consistency. Mix the gelatine and water in a cup and place in a pan of hot water to dissolve. Add to the celery purée with the egg yolk and seasonings. Whisk the egg white until very stiff and fold into the cheese and celery mixture. Spoon into a small mould or into four individual moulds and place in the fridge to set. Turn out to serve and garnish with slices of lemon.

Caviar and Cream Cheese Mousse on Fried Bread

This is another favourite dinner-party starter. If you are on a low-fat diet use quark in place of cream cheese. It won't be quite as velvety but it's still very good.

2 oz/50 g ($\frac{1}{4}$ cup) lumpfish caviar
4 oz/100 g ($\frac{1}{2}$ cup) cream cheese
$\frac{1}{2}$ pint/300 ml (1$\frac{1}{4}$ cups) double (heavy) cream, lightly whipped
freshly ground black pepper
pinch of grated nutmeg
juice of 1 lemon
$\frac{1}{4}$ oz/10 g gelatine
$\frac{1}{4}$ pint/150 ml ($\frac{2}{3}$ cup) strong fish stock
4 circles white bread
butter

Garnish
lemon wedges
fresh dill

Oil four small ramekin dishes. Spoon caviar into the bottom of each mould and chill. Beat together the cream cheese and whipped cream. Add pepper, nutmeg and lemon juice. Soak the gelatine in the fish stock in a small pan. Carefully warm till clear. Mix into the cream cheese mixture and spoon into the moulds. Chill for at least an hour. Very gently fry the rounds of bread in butter until they are light gold in colour and crisp. Drain on kitchen paper and leave to cool. To serve, turn out the moulds on to the rounds of fried bread. Garnish with lemon wedges and dill.

Smoked Salmon Mousse

This is a good way of making a small amount of smoked salmon go a long way.

3 oz/75 g ($\frac{1}{2}$ cup) smoked salmon, finely minced

2 oz/50 g ($\frac{1}{4}$ cup) quark low-fat soft cheese

1 tablespoon mayonnaise

1 large egg (size 1), separated

salt and pepper

$\frac{1}{4}$ oz/8 g gelatine

1$\frac{1}{2}$ tablespoons white wine

Mix the smoked salmon with the quark and then beat in the mayonnaise and the egg yolk. Season to taste. Mix the gelatine with the white wine in a cup and place the cup in a pan of hot water. When the gelatine has dissolved mix with the smoked salmon mixture. Whisk the egg white until it is very stiff and fold into the smoked salmon mixture. Spoon into four individual ramekin dishes and place in the fridge to set.

Herrings in Cream Cheese

This used to be a favourite snack when herrings were more abundant than they are today. It can be made with salt herring fillets or with Bismarck herrings. Remember to leave time to soak the herrings.

8 small salt herring fillets or Bismarck herrings

1 dessert apple, cored and grated

2$\frac{1}{2}$ tablespoons (3$\frac{1}{2}$ tbsp) lemon juice

2 oz/50 g ($\frac{1}{4}$ cup) cream cheese

$\frac{1}{4}$ pint/150 ml ($\frac{2}{3}$ cup) single (light) cream

freshly chopped chives and parsley

Soak the salt herring fillets or Bismarcks in cold water for 12 hours. Keep the onions, if any, from the Bismarcks on one side. When you come to make the dish chop the onions and mix with the grated apple and $\frac{1}{2}$ tablespoon lemon juice. Spread the mixture over the herring fillets. Roll up and arrange on a serving plate. Mix the cream cheese with the remaining lemon juice and the single cream. Beat to a smooth consistency, adding a little milk if the mixture is too thick. Stir in the chosen herbs and pour over the herrings.

Avocado with Shrimps in Cream Cheese Sauce

The use of fresh cheese and relish in this recipe gives a piquant flavour to avocado and prawns.

1 × 6½ oz/185 g can (1 cup) shrimps or 6 oz/175 g (1 cup) peeled prawns

2 oz/50 g (⅔ cup) cream cheese or quark low-fat soft cheese

1 tablespoon mayonnaise

1 tablespoon relish

1 tablespoon cream

salt and pepper

2 avocados, halved and stoned

Drain and wash the canned shrimps. Gradually blend the cheese with the mayonnaise, and then with the relish and cream. Add the shrimps or prawns and season to taste. Fill the centres of the avocados with this mixture. Serve at once with brown bread and butter.

Kipper Pâté

The fresh cheese in this recipe helps to tone down the strength of flavour in the fish. The pâté can be made with any kind of fresh cheese, and smoked mackerel fillets, sardines or pilchards can be substituted for the cooked kipper fillets.

6 oz/175 g kipper fillets, cooked as directed on the pack, and drained

3 oz/75 g (⅔ cup) fresh cheese

1 oz/25 g (1½ tbsp) butter, melted

2 teaspoons lemon juice

black pepper

Remove any skin and bones from the fish. Place all the ingredients together in a blender or food processor and blend until smooth. If you do not have a food processor or blender, mash the fish very well with a fork and then beat in the remaining ingredients. Make sure that everything is well mixed. Spoon into a small pâté dish and chill in the fridge for an hour before serving with fingers of hot toast.

Aubergine with Three Cheeses

This recipe comes from the Provence region of Southern France.

2 lb/900 g aubergines
salt
3–4 tablespoons ($\frac{1}{3}$ cup) olive oil
6 oz/175 g ($\frac{3}{4}$ cup) curd cheese or quark
4 oz/100 g (1 cup) Gruyère cheese, grated
2 oz/50 g ($\frac{1}{2}$ cup) Parmesan cheese, grated
black pepper
4 tablespoons ($\frac{1}{3}$ cup) tomato purée
$\frac{1}{4}$ pint/150 ml ($\frac{2}{3}$ cup) water

Top and tail the aubergines and cut into slices. Lay out flat in a colander and sprinkle with salt. Leave to stand for 30 minutes. Wash very well in cold water and press out all the water. Dry each slice of aubergine on kitchen paper, then brown on each side in hot oil. Place half the slices in a layer in a heatproof entrée dish. Dot with pieces of curd cheese or teaspoons of quark and sprinkle with half the Gruyère and Parmesan. Season with salt and pepper and add a second layer of aubergines. Sprinkle with the remaining cheese and season again. Mix the tomato purée with the water and pour down the sides of the dish. Bake at 180°C/350°F/Gas 4 for 45 minutes. Finish off under the grill to bubble and crust the cheese, and serve with crusty bread.

Cream Cheese and Carrot Soup

This is a favourite winter soup of mine. In fact cream cheese can be used to finish off any creamed vegetable soup.

1 onion, sliced
cooking oil
2 fl. oz/50 ml ($\frac{1}{4}$ cup) dry sherry
12 oz/350 g (3 cups) carrots, sliced
$\frac{1}{2}$ head celery, trimmed
1$\frac{1}{2}$ pints/900 ml (3$\frac{1}{2}$ cups) vegetable stock or water
1 bay leaf
salt and pepper
3 oz/75 g ($\frac{2}{3}$ cup) cream cheese

Fry the onion gently in a little cooking oil. Add the sherry and bring to the boil. Add the carrots and celery to the pan with the stock, bay leaf and seasoning. Bring to the boil, cover and simmer for 1 hour. Remove the bay leaf and blend or sieve the cooked soup with the cream cheese. return to the pan to reheat. Correct seasoning and serve.

Chilled Prawn Bisque

The secret of success with this recipe is only to heat the soup sufficiently to melt the cheese. This ensures that the prawns remain tender. Serve puréed if preferred.

$\frac{1}{2}$ oz/15 g (2 level tsps) butter
1 small onion, finely chopped
8 oz/225 g (1$\frac{1}{3}$ cups) peeled prawns (shrimps)
1 pint/600 ml (2$\frac{1}{2}$ cups) chicken stock
4 oz/100 g ($\frac{1}{2}$ cup) full-fat soft cheese
salt and pepper

Heat the butter in a pan and gently fry the onion for 2–3 minutes to soften. Add prawns and stock. Cut the cheese into small chunks and add to the soup with the seasoning. Remove from the heat and leave to cool. Chill before serving.

Iced Cucumber and Mint Soup

Use fresh mint if you can for this recipe. It is much nicer than dried mint.

½ chicken stock cube
½ pint/300 ml (1¼ cups) boiling water
1 cucumber
8 oz/225 g (1 cup) quark or fromage frais
¼ pint/150 ml (⅔ cup) single (light) cream
1 tablespoon freshly chopped mint
salt and black pepper
ice cubes
paprika pepper

Make up the chicken stock by dissolving the half chicken cube in boiling water. Leave to cool. Grate the cucumber into a large bowl. Stir in all the remaining ingredients, and place in the fridge to chill for at least an hour before serving. Ladle into individual serving bowls, add an ice cube or two and sprinkle with paprika. Serve at once.

MAIN COURSE DISHES

Paneer with Spinach

If you like a really hot curry, use a Madras or Vindaloo curry powder or add ground chilli powder.

5 oz/150 g (1½ cups) paneer (see page 173), cut into small squares
3 tablespoons (¼ cup) cooking oil
2 garlic cloves, peeled and crushed
1 inch/2.5 cm fresh root ginger, grated
1 teaspoon garam marsala or mild curry powder
pinch of cayenne pepper
salt
1 lb/450 g frozen chopped and creamed spinach

Fry the paneer cubes in 2 tablespoons of cooking oil in a non-stick pan until golden brown all over. Remove from the pan and keep on one side. Add the rest of the oil with the garlic and ginger, and fry for 1 minute.

Add all the remaining ingredients and cook over a low heat to thaw the spinach. When the mixture returns to the boil, carefully add the paneer and simmer for a further 5 minutes before serving with boiled rice.

Paneer with Peas

Paneer forms the protein base for some good Indian vegetarian curries.

5 oz/150 g (1½ cups) paneer (see page 173), cut into small squares, with its whey
3 tablespoons (¼ cup) cooking oil
1 medium onion, very finely chopped
1 inch/2.5 cm fresh root ginger, peeled and grated
1 tablespoon ground coriander
1 teaspoon ground cumin
¼ teaspoon turmeric
4 tomatoes, peeled and coarsely chopped
salt and black pepper
8 oz/225 g (½ lb) frozen peas

Fry the paneer cubes in 2 tablespoons of cooking oil in a non-stick pan until golden brown all over. Remove from the pan and keep on one side. Add the rest of the oil with the onion and ginger, and fry until lightly browned. Stir in the spices and then the tomatoes. Cover with the paneer whey and bring to the boil. Simmer for 30 minutes. Add the seasoning and peas and return to the boil. Carefully add the fried paneer and simmer for 5 minutes before serving with boiled rice.

Serbian Stuffed Peppers

This recipe makes a change from those which use rice and meat. Use flavoured cottage cheese for a change.

4 small green or red peppers

Filling
6 oz/175 g (¾ cup) cottage cheese
6 eggs
salt and pepper

Cut the tops off the peppers and scoop out all the seeds and membrane. Mix the cottage cheese with a fork and then beat in the eggs and seasoning. Fill each pepper with some of this mixture. Place in an oiled heatproof dish or tin, and bake at 190°C/375°F/Gas 5 for 1 hour.

Crespolini

This pancake recipe makes quite a substantial dish to serve as a main course. Make half quantity and much smaller pancakes if you want to serve it as a starter.

Pancakes
4 oz/100 g (⅔ cup) flour
pinch of salt
1 egg
½ pint/300 ml (1 cup) milk

Filling
8 oz/225 g (½ lb) frozen chopped spinach, thawed and squeezed dry
8 oz/225 g (1 cup) cream or cottage cheese
2 eggs
2 oz/50 g (⅓ cup) Parmesan cheese, grated

Sauce and topping
2 oz/50 g (¼ cup) butter
2 oz/50 g (⅓ cup) flour
1½ pints/900 ml (3½ cups) milk
salt and pepper
2 oz/50 g (⅓ cup) Bel Paese, cut into slices
1 oz/25 g (2 tbsp) Parmesan cheese, grated

Sieve the flour and salt into a bowl, and beat in the egg and milk. Use the mixture to make about eight pancakes.

Mix all the filling ingredients together and divide between the eight pancakes. Roll them up and tuck in the ends. Place two filled pancakes on each of four heat-proof serving dishes.

Make the sauce by melting the butter and stirring in the flour and milk. Whisk with a wire whisk as the mixture comes to the boil and thickens. Season to taste and pour over the pancakes. Top with slices of Bel Paese and sprinkle with Parmesan. Bake at 200°C/400°F/Gas 6 for about 20 minutes until the dish is lightly browned and bubbly.

Cream Cheese Risotto

This is a very quick risotto recipe. Flavour it with any cold cooked meat, fish or vegetables to hand.

6 oz/175 g ($\frac{3}{4}$ cup) risotto or medium-grain rice
salt
12 fl. oz/350 ml (2 cups) water
1 onion, chopped
1 tablespoon cooking oil
6 oz/175 g (1$\frac{1}{2}$ cups) mixed cooked vegetables (carrots, peas, sweetcorn etc, diced if necessary)
6 oz/175 g (1 cup) cooked ham or chicken, diced
3 oz/75 g ($\frac{1}{3}$ cup) cream or full-fat soft cheese
2–3 tablespoons ($\frac{1}{4}$ cup) milk
freshly ground black pepper

Cook the rice in the salted boiling water for 12–15 minutes until the rice is tender and all the liquid has been absorbed. (Add a little more water if the liquid is absorbed in 12 minutes.) Fry the onion in cooking oil until soft, then add the cooked vegetables and meat and mix well. Heat thoroughly and then add the cooked rice. Cream the cheese with the milk and pour over the risotto mixture. Heat through, season to taste with salt and pepper, and serve with a green salad.

Curd Cheese and Herb Tart

This makes a very light fluffy flan which makes a nice change from the heavier quiches.

1 × 7½ oz/215 g (½ lb) packet frozen shortcrust pastry, thawed
2 bunches spring onions (scallions), trimmed and roughly chopped
1 oz/25 g (1½ tbsp) butter
1 teaspoon olive oil
1 bunch watercress, trimmed and chopped
2 tablespoons (3 tbsp) freshly chopped parsley
2 tablespoons (3 tbsp) freshly chopped chives
pinch of mixed dried herbs
5 oz/150 g (⅔ cup) curd cheese
3 eggs, separated
1 tablespoon milk
salt and freshly ground black pepper

Roll out the pastry and use to line an 8 inch/20 cm loose-based flan tin. Prick the base very well all over and bake blind (with beans, greaseproof or foil) at 190°C/375°F/Gas 5 for 10 minutes. Meanwhile gently fry the spring onions in the butter and olive oil. After 2–3 minutes add the watercress and herbs and cook for a further 2–3 minutes. Remove the pastry case from the oven. Prick again with a fork and spread the onion and herb mixture all over the base. Mix the curd cheese, egg yolks and milk to a smooth paste, and season. Whisk the egg whites stiffly and fold into the cheese and yolk mixture and spoon into the flan. Return to the oven and bake for 35–40 minutes until well risen and lightly browned on top. Serve warm or cold.

Cod Capri

The cream cheese here gives a really creamy finish to the fish.

1 lb/450 g white fish fillets (cod, whiting, haddock or huss), skinned and boned

3 oz/75 g ($\frac{1}{3}$ cup) cream cheese

1 tablespoon cooking oil

1 onion, sliced

4 oz/100 g (1$\frac{1}{4}$ cups) mushrooms, sliced

salt and pepper

3 tomatoes, skinned and sliced

$\frac{1}{2}$ teaspoon mixed dried herbs

Cut the fish and the cheese into cubes and arrange in the base of an ovenproof dish. Heat the oil in a frying pan and gently fry the onion for 2–3 minutes until it turns transparent. Add the mushrooms and continue cooking for a further 2–3 minutes. Spoon this mixture over the fish, and season well. Top with slices of tomato and sprinkle with mixed herbs. Cover with a lid or with foil and bake at 180°C/350°F/Gas 4 for 35–40 minutes.

Cheesy Herb Chicken

The cheesy layer beneath the skin flavours the chicken and also helps to stop the breast meat drying out.

1 × 4 lb/1.8 kg roasting chicken

5 tablespoons (6 tbsp) quark or fromage frais

1 tablespoon freshly chopped parsley

1 teaspoon freshly chopped tarragon or $\frac{1}{4}$ teaspoon dried tarragon

pinch of dried mixed herbs

salt and freshly ground black pepper

Wash and dry the chicken and then carefully ease away the skin from the flesh over the breast and the top of the thighs, taking care not to break or tear the skin. Mix the quark or fromage frais with the herbs and seasoning and push in between the exposed flesh and the skin. Gently pull the skin back into place and wrap the bird in foil. Roast it at 190°C/375°F/Gas 5 for 1 hour. Remove the foil and return to the oven for a further 20–30 minutes to finish off the chicken and brown the skin.

Creamy Chicken Casserole

The cream cheese in this recipe makes a really creamy sauce with no fuss.

4 chicken joints, skinned and cut into 2 pieces each
1 medium onion, sliced
1 cooking apple, peeled, cored and sliced
1 oz/25 g (2 tbsp) raisins
salt and pepper
¾ pint/450 ml (2 cups) chicken stock
3 oz/75 g (⅓ cup) cream or full-fat soft cheese
3 teaspoons (1 tbsp) cornflour (cornstarch)
2 tablespoons (3 tbsp) milk

Place the chicken joints in a casserole and add the onion, apple, raisins and seasoning. Pour on the stock, cover and cook at 190°C/375°F/Gas 5 for 1 hour until the chicken is tender. Cream the cheese and then mix the cornflour with the milk. Blend into the cheese. Spoon a few tablespoonfuls of the hot cooking liquor from the casserole into the cheese mixture and stir. Pour all the cheese mixture into the casserole and stir. Return the casserole to the oven for 20 minutes until the sauce has thickened.

ACCOMPANIMENTS AND SALADS

Leeks in Cream Cheese Sauce

This dish can be made with any kind of fresh cheese.

1½ lb/675 g leeks, trimmed and sliced
salt
4 rashers streaky (Canadian) bacon
4 oz/100 g (½ cup) cream cheese or quark
freshly ground black pepper

Cook the leeks in a very little lightly salted water for about 10–15 minutes until tender. Grill the bacon until crisp and cut into small pieces. Keep on one side. When the leeks are cooked check the water level. There should only be about 2–3 tablespoons of water in the bottom of the pan. Drain off any excess and return to the heat. Add the cream cheese or quark and stir over a low heat until it all melts into the cooking liquid. Add the bacon and black pepper and bring to the boil. Serve at once.

Soufflé Potatoes

This dish is almost a meal in itself. To serve as a main course increase the quantities or serve with rashers of bacon on top and a green salad.

1 lb/450 g floury potatoes, peeled and cut into quarters
salt
2 oz/50 g ($\frac{1}{4}$ cup) butter
4 oz/100 g ($\frac{1}{2}$ cup) quark or fromage frais
2 large eggs, separated

Cook the potatoes in lightly salted boiling water until tender. Take care that they do not 'fall' into the water. Drain well and mash with butter and a little more salt. Beat in the cheese and then the egg yolks. Whisk the egg whites until they are very stiff and mix 2 tablespoonfuls into the potato mixture. Fold in the rest of the egg whites and spoon the mixture into a greased soufflé dish. Bake at 200°C/400°F/Gas 6 for 20–25 minutes until well risen and golden brown on top. Serve at once.

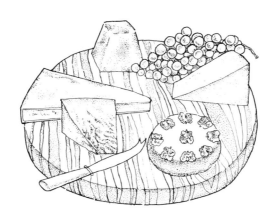

Crowdie Potato Cakes

It's worth cooking the potatoes specially to make this Scottish favourite.

1 lb/450 g mashed potatoes
1 egg yolk
2 oz/50 g ($\frac{1}{4}$ cup) Crowdie cheese
1 oz/25 g ($1\frac{1}{2}$ tbsp) butter
1 tablespoon freshly chopped chives
salt and pepper
butter or cooking oil for frying

Mix the mashed potato with the egg yolk, cheese, butter and chives and season to taste. Shape into small but thick round flat cakes and fry in hot fat for about 3–4 minutes on each side. The cakes should be crisp and golden in colour.

Curd Cheese Dumplings

Dumplings are very popular in Eastern Europe. This recipe comes from Hungary. Serve with stews in place of potatoes.

4 oz/100 g ($\frac{2}{3}$ cup) flour
$\frac{1}{2}$ teaspoon baking powder
6 oz/175 g ($\frac{3}{4}$ cup) curd cheese
$\frac{1}{2}$ teaspoon mixed herbs
ground black pepper
1 egg

Mix the flour, baking powder, curd cheese, mixed herbs and pepper together. Beat the egg and add to the dry ingredients to give a smooth dough. Roll the dough, using floured hands, into eight equal balls. Cook the dumplings by gently poaching them uncovered in well flavoured stock or in a stew liquid for 20 minutes.

DESSERTS AND BAKING

Apple Batter Pudding

This is rather like a sweet toad-in-the-hole with a slightly runny centre! It's delicious.

4 oz/100 g ($\frac{2}{3}$ cup) flour

1 egg

2 oz/50 g ($\frac{1}{4}$ cup) cream cheese or quark

$\frac{1}{2}$ pint/300 ml (1$\frac{1}{4}$ cups) milk

2 tablespoons sugar

butter

1 lb/450 g cooking apples, cored and sliced

Sift the flour into a basin. Make a well in the centre and break in the egg. Mix the cream cheese or quark with a little of the milk to make a smooth cream and gradually add in the rest of the milk. Pour half of the mixture into the basin with the egg. Gradually mix together drawing in flour from the sides, a little at a time. Beat well together and then beat in the rest of the cheesy milk mixture and half the sugar. Place a few knobs of butter in a Yorkshire pudding tin and place in an oven preheated to 230°C/450°F/Gas 8 for a minute or two. Then pour in the batter mixture. Sprinkle with the apples and the remaining sugar. Return to the oven and bake for 1 hour, 10 minutes until golden brown in colour and well puffed up. Cover with greaseproof paper or foil after 30 minutes.

Quark Ice Cream

This is an extremely quick ice cream to make. In the summer you can substitute any kind of sweetened fruit purée for the apple sauce and jam; allow about $\frac{3}{4}$ lb/350 g.

1 × 9$\frac{1}{2}$ oz/270 g ($\frac{1}{2}$ lb) jar apple sauce

3 tablespoons raspberry or strawberry jam or marmalade

8 oz/225 g (1 cup) quark or fromage frais

Mix the apple sauce with the jam or marmalade and sieve. Stir in the quark or fromage frais and beat with a fork. Spoon the mixture into a rigid polythene container and place in the freezer or in the frozen food compartment of the fridge. Leave for at least 4 hours before serving.

157

Summer Fruit Mountains

This is a very popular dessert in Germany where the quark mixture is usually piled up in the centre of a plate and the fruit is arranged round the outside. However this way of serving the dessert in glass dishes also looks very attractive.

¼ pint/150 ml (⅔ cup) double (heavy) cream

2 tablespoons (3 tbsp) Kirsch or any fruit brandy

1 tablespoon sugar

6 oz/175 g (¾ cup) quark or fromage frais

12 oz/350 g (¾ lb) fresh summer fruits such as raspberries, strawberries or sliced peaches

toasted flaked almonds, to decorate

Lightly whip the cream with the liqueur and sugar. Fold into the quark. Spoon a little of the mixture into the base of four wine glasses and then layer with the chosen fruit. Sprinkle with toasted flaked almonds just before serving.

Yorkshire Curd Tarts

In most parts of the country curd tarts are now made without any milk curds at all. However, in Yorkshire the old traditions continue.

1 × 7½ oz/215 g (½ lb) packet frozen shortcrust pastry, thawed

8 oz/225 g (1 cup) curd cheese

2 oz/50 g (¼ cup) sugar

1 tablespoon milk

2 eggs, beaten

2 oz/50 g (⅓ cup) raisins

nutmeg or grated lemon rind

Roll out the pastry and use to line four ovenproof (such as Denby) saucers or six Yorkshire pudding pans. Mix together the curd cheese, sugar and milk, then add the eggs, one at a time. Add the raisins at the end when the mixture is smooth. Spoon on to the pastry and sprinkle with nutmeg or grated lemon rind. Bake at 180°C/350°F/Gas 4 for 30 minutes until the filling is set. Allow an extra 10 minutes if using saucers.

Cheese and Marmalade Tart

Frozen pastry will be even quicker if you are in a hurry.

6 oz/175 g (1 cup) flour
salt
3 oz/75 g ($\frac{1}{3}$ cup) butter
water

Filling
12 oz/350 g (1$\frac{1}{2}$ cups) curd cheese or quark low-fat soft cheese
4 tablespoons ($\frac{1}{3}$ cup) chunky marmalade
3 eggs

To make the pastry, sift the flour and salt into a bowl. Rub in the butter until the mixture resembles fine breadcrumbs. Bind with water. Leave to rest and then roll out and line an 8 inch/20 cm flan tin. Use any remaining pastry to make strips for a criss-cross effect on the top of the tart.

Blend curd cheese and marmalade with a wooden spoon. Whisk the eggs, then whisk into the cheese and orange mixture. Pour into the flan and arrange the pastry strips on the top. Fork the edges and bake in the centre of the oven, preheated to 180°C/350°F/Gas 4, for 1 hour until the centre is firm and the top of the tart is golden brown in colour. Leave to cool.

Quark Fruit Dessert

This can be made with any combination of berries and soft fruit.

1 lb/450 g (2 cups) quark
5 fl. oz/150 ml ($\frac{1}{2}$ cup) double (heavy) cream
4 tablespoons icing sugar, sifted
few drops vanilla essence (optional)
8 oz/225 g ($\frac{1}{2}$ lb) sugared fresh raspberries, redcurrants, blackcurrants, blackberries or strawberries

Whisk the quark, cream and sugar until the mixture is light and frothy. Add the vanilla essence and combine well. Gently stir in the sugared fruit, reserving some for decoration, and spoon mixture into 4 individual serving dishes. Chill before serving.

Fruit and Nut Curd Flan

This is based on the old-fashioned curd tarts but has a Middle-Eastern influence of dried fruit and pine kernels.

1 × 7½ oz/215 g (½ lb) packet frozen shortcrust pastry, thawed

2 oz/50 g (⅓ cup) dates, chopped coarsely

4 oz/100 g (½ cup) dried 'no need to soak' apricots, chopped coarsely

2 eggs

4 oz/100 g (½ cup) quark

3 fl. oz/75 ml (⅓ cup) soured cream

1 tablespoon sugar

2 fl. oz/50 ml (¼ cup) milk

½ oz/15 g (1 tbsp) pine kernels, toasted

Roll out pastry and use to line an 8 inch/20 cm flan tin. Sprinkle the dates and apricots over the base. Mix the eggs, quark, soured cream, sugar and milk together and pour over the top. Sprinkle with toasted pine kernels and bake at 190°C/375°F/Gas 5 for 45 minutes. Serve hot or cold.

Cheesecake

This recipe makes a very much lighter style of cheesecake than the baked ones.

10 digestive biscuits, crushed

1½ oz/40 g (1½ tbsp) butter, melted

1 oz/25 g (1½ tbsp) sugar

1 large orange

a little grated lemon rind

8 oz/225 g (1 cup) cottage cheese

orange juice

1 small packet (1 tbsp) gelatine

Mix the digestive biscuits with the butter and sugar and press into the base of a 7 inch/18 cm loose-based flan tin. Press down very well. Grate the rind from the orange and mix with the lemon rind and cottage cheese.

Right: *Caviar and Cream Cheese Mousse on Fried Bread (page 143) and Chèvre Kiwi Salad (page 124).*

Squeeze the orange and make the juice up to $\frac{1}{2}$ pint/300 ml (1 cup) with more orange juice. Spoon 2 or 3 tablespoonfuls of this over the gelatine and stir in a cup. Place the cup in a pan of hot water and stir until the gelatine dissolves. Blend the rest of the juice with the cottage cheese mixture in a food processor or blender. Failing that, rub the cheese through a sieve and gradually stir in the juice. Stir in the gelatine and pour into the flan base. Place in the fridge and leave to set for at least 2 hours.

Strongbow Cheesecake

This is a light fluffy cheesecake which is very easy to make and there's no baking involved.

4 oz/100 g ($\frac{1}{4}$ lb) plain chocolate digestive biscuits, crushed

2 oz/50 g ($\frac{1}{4}$ cup) butter, melted

1 packet (1 tbsp) gelatine

$\frac{1}{4}$ pint/150 ml ($\frac{2}{3}$ cup) Strongbow cider

8 oz/225 g (1 cup) cottage cheese

4 oz/100 g ($\frac{1}{2}$ cup) cream cheese

1–2 oz/25–50 g ($\frac{1}{4}$–$\frac{1}{2}$ cup) icing sugar

$\frac{1}{4}$ pint/150 ml ($\frac{2}{3}$ cup) double (heavy) cream

Decoration
fresh orange slices

Grease an 8 inch/20 cm spring-clip or loose-bottomed cake tin. Mix the crushed biscuits with the melted butter. Press the mixture over the base of the tin. Dissolve the gelatine in the warmed cider, and leave to cool but not set. Sieve the cottage cheese and cream cheese, then stir in the sugar, cider and gelatine. Beat thoroughly. Whisk the cream until fairly thick and fold into the mixture. Pour over the biscuit base and leave to set. For decoration, arrange slices of fresh orange on top.

Left: *Quark Fruit Dessert (page 159).*

Baked Cheesecake

This is a Jewish recipe. It comes from some old friends who often serve it at the Jewish festival of Shavout *when dairy products are a traditional food. It is not too rich.*

10 digestive biscuits (1½ cups), crushed
2½ oz/65 g (¼ cup) butter, melted
8 oz/225 g (1 cup) cream cheese or full-fat soft cheese
4 oz/100 g (½ cup) sugar
4 eggs, separated
juice of ½ lemon
2 oz/50 g (⅓ cup) flour
½ teaspoon salt
½ teaspoon baking powder

Mix the biscuit crumbs with the melted butter and press into the base of an 8 inch/20 cm loose-based flan tin. Beat the cream cheese with 2 tablespoons of the sugar, the egg yolks and lemon juice. Fold in the flour, salt and baking powder. Whisk the egg whites until stiff and then whisk in the remaining sugar. Gently fold the egg whites into the cheese mixture. Spoon on to the crumb base and bake at 180°C/350°F/Gas 4 for 50–55 minutes until well risen and brown on top. Leave to cool before removing from the tin.

Hot Citrus Cheesecake

In France this is called Gâteau au Fromage Blanc and it is eaten straight from the oven with thick cream.

3 eggs, separated
12 oz/350 g (1½ cups) quark or fromage frais
4 tablespoons (⅓ cup) sugar
grated rind of 1 orange
grated rind of 1 lemon
1½ tablespoons (2 tbsp) candied peel, finely chopped
4 tablespoons (⅓ cup) flour

Mix the egg yolks with the quark and sugar and beat until smooth. Stir in the grated orange and lemon rind, the candied peel and the flour. Whisk the egg whites until they are very stiff and fold into the cheese mixture, one-half at a time. Spoon into a greased 8 inch/20 cm cake tin and bake at 180°C/350°F/Gas 4 for 30 minutes. Cover with foil and Bakewell paper. Increase the heat to 190°C/375°F/Gas 5 and cook for a further 30–45 minutes until cooked through. Leave to cool for 5–10 minutes before removing from the cake tin.

Ecuadorian Cheese Pies

This recipe is one of the many variations on the South American Empanada. The overall effect is fairly sweet, so serve as a dessert with cream or yogurt, or as a teatime snack.

12 oz/350 g (2 cups) flour
$\frac{1}{4}$ teaspoon salt
5 oz/150 g ($\frac{2}{3}$ cup) butter, cut into pieces
1 teaspoon sugar
1 beaten egg
5 tablespoons (6 tbsp) cold water
milk for glazing

Filling
3 oz/75 g ($\frac{1}{2}$ cup) seedless raisins, chopped
2 hard-boiled eggs, chopped
2 oz/50 g ($\frac{1}{4}$ cup) quark or low-fat soft cheese
1 teaspoon sugar

Sift the flour and salt into a bowl and rub into the butter until the mixture resembles fine breadcrumbs. Stir in the sugar and then mix in the beaten egg and water to make a firm dough. Roll out thinly and cut into six squares.

To make the filling, mix all the ingredients together. Place a small heap on each pastry square and fold the pastry over to form triangles. Damp the edges with a little milk and pinch together. Flute the edges with a fork. Transfer to a greased baking tray, brush with milk and bake at 200°C/400°F/Gas 6 for 12–15 minutes until golden in colour. Eat hot or cold.

Peppermint Creams

Cream cheese can be used as the basis for a variety of deliciously creamy tasting sweets. They usually need to be made the day before to allow for a little drying out.

1 oz/25 g (1½ tbsp) cream cheese
8 oz/225 g (2 cups) icing sugar
a few drops of peppermint essence

Place the cream cheese in a basin and add half the sugar and the peppermint essence. Beat with a wooden spoon until very smooth. Add the rest of the sugar and beat again. Sprinkle the work surface with icing sugar and place the cheese mint mixture on this. Sprinkle with more icing sugar and roll out. Use small cutters to cut out rounds or shapes and place in a piece of greaseproof paper which has been sprinkled with icing sugar. Leave to dry out overnight.

Chocolate Cheese Truffles

Truffles always go down well at the end of a good dinner and these are even better than usual. Remember, though, that they need to be made the day before they are required.

Makes 16–20

4 oz/100 g (½ cup) cream cheese
8 oz/225 g (2 cups) icing sugar
2 oz/50 g (⅓ cup) cocoa powder
1 oz/25 g (1½ tbsp) glacé cherries, chopped
1 oz/25 g (2 tbsp) raisins, chopped
1 oz/25 g (¼ cup) ground almonds
chocolate vermicelli

Place the cream cheese in a basin, sift in the icing sugar and cocoa, and beat until smooth. Add the glacé cherries, raisins and ground almonds and mix in. Place the mixture in the fridge and leave to chill for 2 hours. Shape the mixture into sixteen to twenty small balls and roll in chocolate vermicelli. Leave to stand for 2 hours and then return to the fridge. Serve the next day.

Coconut Ice

This is simplicity itself to make, and quite delicious.

2 oz/50 g ($\frac{1}{4}$ cup) cream cheese
8 oz/225 g (2 cups) icing sugar
3 oz/75 g ($\frac{3}{4}$ cup) desiccated coconut
a few drops of red food colouring

Place the cream cheese in a basin and sift in the icing sugar. Beat well together until smooth and creamy. Add the coconut and mix again. Spread half the mixture into a 6 inch/15 cm square on a baking tray or in a Swiss roll tin. Place in the fridge for 30 minutes. Meanwhile mix a few drops of red food colouring into the remaining mixture. Spread this over the top of the white square and return to the fridge for a further 30 minutes. Cut into squares to serve.

Cottage Cheese Loaf

Serve buttered and sliced with salads and supper dishes.

12 oz/350 g (2 cups) self-raising flour
$\frac{1}{2}$ teaspoon salt
$\frac{1}{4}$ teaspoon dry mustard powder
pinch of cayenne pepper
2 oz/50 g ($\frac{1}{4}$ cup) butter
6 tablespoons ($\frac{1}{2}$ cup) milk
1 egg, beaten
4 oz/100 g ($\frac{1}{2}$ cup) cottage cheese, sieved
pinch of dried mixed herbs

Sift the flour, salt, dry mustard and cayenne into a mixing bowl. Cut the butter into small pieces and rub into the dry ingredients. Mix the milk and egg with the cottage cheese and herbs and pour over the dry ingredients. Mix to a soft dough. Turn out on to a floured board and knead lightly until smooth. Place the dough in a 1 lb/450 g loaf tin and bake at 180°C/350°F/Gas 4 for 1$\frac{1}{4}$ hours until golden brown. Turn out and leave to cool on a wire rack.

Ginger Marmalade Loaf

Add a little more ginger to this recipe if you like a really fierce gingery flavour.

4 oz/100 g ($\frac{1}{2}$ cup) butter
3 tablespoons ($\frac{1}{4}$ cup) marmalade
4 oz/100 g ($\frac{1}{2}$ cup) sugar
4 oz/100 g ($\frac{1}{2}$ cup) cottage cheese
8 oz/225 g (1$\frac{1}{3}$ cups) self-raising flour
1 teaspoon ground ginger
2 eggs, beaten
1 tablespoon milk

Heat the butter, marmalade and sugar in a pan until the butter and sugar melt. Do not allow the mixture to boil. Sieve the cottage cheese and place in a bowl with the flour and ginger. Leave the marmalade mixture to cool a little, and then beat in the eggs. Pour over the dry ingredients, and mix to a smooth consistency. Line and grease a 1 lb/450 g loaf tin. Pour the mixture into the loaf tin and bake at 180°C/350°F/Gas 4 for 1 hour. Test with a skewer. If it comes out clean the cake is cooked. Turn on to a wire rack to cool.

Cheese Icing for Cakes

This makes the most delicious filling and topping for Passion Cake and American Carrot Cake and there is no reason why it should not also be used on other cakes. Use one of the flavourings only!

3 oz/75 g ($\frac{1}{3}$ cup) cream cheese
3 oz/75 g ($\frac{1}{3}$ cup) soft butter
6 oz/175 g (1$\frac{1}{2}$ cups) icing sugar, sifted

Flavourings
$\frac{1}{2}$ teaspoon grated lemon rind, orange rind, or Camp Coffee

Place the cheese, butter and sugar together in a bowl and add your chosen flavouring. Beat well with a wooden spoon until the mixture is soft and creamy and the flavourings are well mixed in. Use part of the mixture as a filling for the cake and use the rest to coat the whole cake. Use a fork to give a roughened effect or decorate with chopped nuts, coloured vermicelli or other cake decorations.

Boursin Biscuits

This is a delicious way to use up Boursin. The biscuits are really short and crisp. You can also use other flavoured cream cheeses such as Herb and Garlic Roulés. These do not have quite the fat content of Boursin so increase the butter or margarine in the recipe to 3 oz/75 g.

Makes 16

5 oz/150 g ($\frac{3}{4}$ cup) wholemeal flour
3 oz/75 g ($\frac{1}{2}$ cup) medium oatmeal
$\frac{1}{4}$ teaspoon salt
2 oz/50 g ($\frac{1}{4}$ cup) butter or margarine
3 oz/75 g ($\frac{1}{3}$ cup) Boursin or similar cheese

Mix flour, oatmeal and salt in a bowl. Cut the butter or margarine into small pieces and rub into the dry ingredients until the mixture resembles breadcrumbs. Bind with the cheese and mix to a stiff dough. Roll out on a floured surface and cut into sixteen biscuits, $2\frac{1}{2}$–3 inches/6–7 cm in diameter. Place on a greased baking tray and bake at 200°C/400°F/Gas 6 for 12–15 minutes. Carefully transfer to a wire rack and leave to cool.

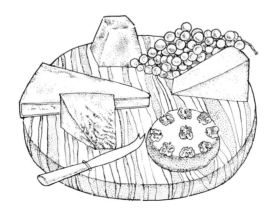

When milk sours it separates into curds and whey, caused by bacterial action which produces lactic acid, and this separation is the first step in any kind of cheese-making. In the past untreated milk could be left to sour quickly simply by leaving it to stand at room temperature. However, most of us do not have our own cows and therefore have to buy pasteurised milk from the supermarket. This milk is more likely to go 'off' than to sour, and it will take some time to do even this. The 'off' flavours come from the action of *unwanted* bacteria.

So, to make cheese at home, you will need either to induce curdling by the use of an acid material such as vinegar or lemon juice, or you will need to use a 'starter culture'. One of the easiest starter cultures to use is cultured buttermilk. Though the milk will form into curds and whey on its own, the more sophisticated cheeses use rennet to coagulate the milk. Rennet produces a much thicker and firmer curd which has to be cut to release the whey. Some cheeses are cooked at this stage, for the addition of heat accelerates the removal of the whey.

The next stage in the cheese-making process is to press the cheese and compact it into a solid unit. The pressure needed to do this varies from cheese to cheese. Fresh cheeses like cottage cheese and cream cheese need not be pressed at all.

The final stage in the making of hard cheeses and soft matured cheeses is the ripening time. Again the optimum ripening time varies from cheese to cheese. Parmesan and Cheddar, for example, are not at their peak until nearly a year has passed, whereas cottage cheese should be eaten as soon as possible after making.

Unless you are thinking of becoming a really dedicated cheese-maker only the simplest of cheeses are worth attempting at home. The more sophisticated cheeses require some kind of double cooker, large moulds and presses, none of which are very easy to improvize. You also need to work with quite large quantities of milk. A gallon (4.5 litres) is the minimum quantity and some cheeses are simply not worth making with less than 5 or 10 gallons (22–45 litres). This is partly because about 95 per cent of the water held in milk is released in cheese-making – this greatly reduces the volume of the finished cheese – and also because of curing problems encountered with very small quantities of cheese.

The texture of the cheese you make will depend partly on the type of milk you start with – the fatter the milk the creamier the cheese – and on how long you heat it or hang it. Over-heating can result in a very grainy cheese and over-hanging will dry the cheese out.

To hang the cheese, pour the curd into muslin, gather up the corners and tie with string. This bag can be hung from the bars of an upturned tall stool, from a mixer tap overnight, or from a special stand, such as those described below.

The amount of cheese made will vary, obviously, but generally speaking 1 lb/450 g yogurt or 2 pints/1.2 litres will make about 5–6 oz/150–175 g.

Equipment Needed for Simple Cheese-Making

1 large saucepan and 1 double saucepan
large bowls
plenty of muslin
1 large colander
1 sugar thermometer
nylon sieves of various sizes
$4\frac{1}{2}$ inch/11 cm plastic tubs with holes cut in the base

You can buy a very useful yogurt and soft

cheese-maker set and a jelly bag stand – very useful for cheese – from Lakeland Plastics of Windermere.

Hygiene

Hygiene is of paramount importance in all cheese-making. All equipment should be as clean as possible and this means scalding or boiling it. Drainage cloths, in particular, must be carefully washed and boiled. Avoid the use of strong detergents, especially on wooden implements, which could take up the flavour and pass it on to the cheese.

You will probably be making your cheese in the kitchen and you are unlikely to have flowers in the room. But fruit should also be removed and you should avoid making bread or wine at the same time or just before making the cheese. This is to ensure that no undesirable yeasts get into the cheese.

Yogurt Cheese

This must be the easiest kind of all cheese to make for the yogurt already contains its own 'starter', being a cultured product. Yogurt Cheese has a much stronger acid flavour than mild cheeses like Yorkshire Curd Cheese. Both cow's and goat's milk yogurt can be used.

The best kind of yogurt for cheese-making is a fairly firmly set, home-made yogurt. However commercial brands can be used, but make sure that they are well set: the very runny ones tend to run through the muslin.

1 lb/450 g yogurt, cow's or goat's

Line a large sieve with a square of muslin and spoon the yogurt into it. Gather up the corners of the square and tie with string. Hang to drip over a bowl. Alternatively use a yogurt or cheese-maker. Leave to drip for about 20–24 hours. This gives a really soft and smooth spreadable cheese. The cheese can be further pressed by spooning into a small nylon sieve lined with muslin. Place a large weight wrapped in clingfilm on top and place the sieve over a basin. Leave for 24–36 hours to get a smooth firm cheese which can be cut into wedges.

Labneh

This Lebanese dish is also called Dried Yogurt and is really the halfway stage between yogurt and yogurt cheese. Simply remove the contents of the muslin bag a little earlier.

Kariesch

This recipe is reputed to have come from the nomads of Central Asia. It makes a less creamy cheese than some of the others because it is made with non-fat milk.

2 pints/1.2 litres (5 cups) cultured buttermilk

Pour the buttermilk into the top of a double saucepan and heat gently to about 38°C/100°F. Remove from the heat and leave to stand for about 30 minutes. Line a large nylon sieve standing over a bowl with muslin. Pour in the buttermilk. Lift out the cloth and tie the corners. Hang up over the bowl for 6 hours. Put a clean piece of muslin in the sieve and press the cheese in this. Leave to drain for a few more hours and turn out.

Yorkshire Curd Cheese

Use this cheese to make Yorkshire Curd Tarts and Cheesecake. It's also very good salted and served with salad and wholemeal rolls.

2 pints/1.2 litres (5 cups) milk
juice of 3 lemons, strained

Put the milk and lemon juice in a bowl and leave to stand in a warm place or an airing cupboard for about 12 hours or overnight. Put a large piece of muslin over another bowl and pour the curds into this. Tie with string and hang to dry. When the bag has stopped dripping, (about 24 hours), scrape the curd from the muslin and use for cooking or salt lightly to taste and pack into a small container. Cover with muslin and press with a weight. Eat within 2 or 3 days.

Cottage Cheese I

This cottage cheese is fairly crumbly and if you mix it with a little yogurt is rather like the American style cottage cheese. It has a mildly acid flavour. It is very good mixed with freshly chopped herbs or with caraway seeds.

2 pints/1.2 litres (5 cups) milk
2 tablespoons (3 tbsp) wine or cider vinegar
salt

Pour the milk into a pan and heat it to the point where it begins to bubble and rise in the pan. Add the vinegar and stir well. Remove the milk from the heat and leave to stand for 4 hours. Strain the whey through muslin over a bowl, leaving the curd to drip for about 14–16 hours until the drips have stopped. Season and flavour to taste.

Cottage Cheese II

This takes a little longer to coagulate and the separation of the curds and whey is helped by the addition of heat. The result is rather like quark or traditional British cottage cheese.

2 pints/1.2 litres (5 cups) skimmed milk
4 tablespoons (5 tbsp) cultured buttermilk

Heat the milk to 32°C/90°F and pour into a large thermos flask. Stir in the buttermilk and cover with the lid. Leave to stand for 24 hours. Carefully transfer the milk to the top half of a double saucepan and gently heat to separate the curds and whey. Strain the curd into a piece of muslin in a colander over a bowl. Tie up the corners and hang up to drip for 12–16 hours.

Semi-Hard Cottage Cheese

10–12 oz/300–350 g ($\frac{3}{4}$ lb) home-made cottage cheese
salt
vine leaves or dock leaves

Line two small nylon sieves or small plastic pots (with drainage holes cut in the base) with muslin. Mix the cottage cheese with salt. Spoon half of the cheese into each one. Cover with muslin and top each one with a heavy weight covered in clingfilm. When the cheeses are firm enough to hold their shape, turn out and wrap in the leaves. Tie with string. Leave the cheeses on a wire rack to dry, turning the cheeses each day. When the leaves are completely dry, keep in the fridge or freezer until ready to use.

Paneer or Indian Curd Cheese

Paneer is the Indian name for cheese made from milk which is curdled by heating with lemon juice. It has a very mild flavour.

2 pints/1.2 litres (5 cups) milk
juice of 1 lemon, sieved

Pour the milk into a saucepan and bring to the boil. Add the lemon juice and stir. Carry on cooking for a minute or so until the milk is thoroughly curdled. Remove from the heat and leave to cool. Turn into a large piece of double muslin and hang over a bowl until all the whey has dripped through. Keep the whey to use as stock. The curds will be quite dry and firm after about 4 hours. Remove the muslin and flatten the curds. Place on a plate with a heavy weight on top. Leave for another couple of hours or so. This treatment firms up the curds so that you can cut them into small squares for Paneer curries (see pages 148 and 149).

Colwick Cheese

Makeshift moulds can be made by cutting holes in the base of large plastic ice cream tubs. This cheese is characterized by its depressed centre and curled over edges.

4 pints/2.5 litres (10 cups) milk
1 tablespoon cultured buttermilk
1 tablespoon junket rennet
½–1 oz/15–25 g salt
walnut halves

Heat the milk to 68°C/155°F and then cool to 32°C/90°F. Add the cultured buttermilk and rennet and stir well. Leave to stand in a warm place for 1 hour. Line a mould made as suggested above with squares of muslin, or line a large nylon sieve. Cut thin slices of curd and use to fill up the moulds. After 2 hours pull the corners of the muslin into the middle and tie tightly with string. Every 2 hours for 12 hours, squeeze the cheese and retie the muslin. Leave to drain for 2 days until the muslin can be peeled off leaving a firm cheese. Sprinkle with salt and leave to dry. Store in the fridge and eat within 5–6 days. Serve with walnut halves in the depressed centre.

Crowdie

*This soft creamy cheese from
Scotland has double cream added at
the end. It is delicious served with
fresh pineapple.*

3 pints/1.8 litres (7½ cups) milk

3 teaspoons (1 tbsp) junket rennet or 1 teaspoon cheese rennet

1 tablespoon double (heavy) cream

salt

Warm the milk to about 32°C/90°F and add the rennet.
Stir well and leave to stand for 4 hours. Cut the curd
into cubes and leave in a warm place for another 4 hours.
Drain the curd through muslin for about 16 hours. The
texture will be very soft, rather like quark. Remove
the curd from the muslin and place in a bowl. Stir in
the double cream and salt to taste, and mix to a soft
creamy paste.

Cream Cheese

*The richness of the cream cheese
will depend upon the type of cream
you use. Whipping cream produces
a product rather like Petit Suisse.*

2 pints/1.2 litres (5 cups) single (light) or whipping cream

2 teaspoons cultured buttermilk

2 teaspoons junket rennet or 1 teaspoon cheese rennet diluted
   in 4 teaspoons water

salt

pinhead oatmeal, toasted

Heat the cream in a double pan to 79°C/175°F and then
cool to 27°C/80°F. Stir in the buttermilk and rennet
and leave to stand in a warm place overnight. Next
morning ladle slices of coagulated cream into muslin
and hang up to drain. Leave to hang for 2 days, scraping
the curd from the cloth into the centre every 6 hours,
and changing the cloth halfway through. Salt to taste.
Form into rounds or a small roll and coat with toasted
oatmeal. Store in the fridge and eat within 4–5 days.

ACKNOWLEDGMENTS

The author and the publishers would like to thank the following individuals and organizations for supplying the photographs used in this book.

The London Cheese Company/Michael O'Brien (opposite pages 32 and 33)

James Murphy (opposite page 160)

Cheeses from Switzerland (opposite page 64 and overleaf, and opposite pages 96 and 97)

CMA-German Food and Drink (opposite page 161)

Dairy Crest Foods (opposite page 128)

National Dairy Council (opposite page 65 and overleaf)

Danish Dairy Board (opposite page 129).